WILLIAMS-SONOMA

BARCELONA

AUTHENTIC RECIPES CELEBRATING THE FOODS OF THE WORLD

Recipes and Text
PAUL RICHARDSON

Photographs
JASON LOWE

General Editor
CHUCK WILLIAMS

Oxmoor
House

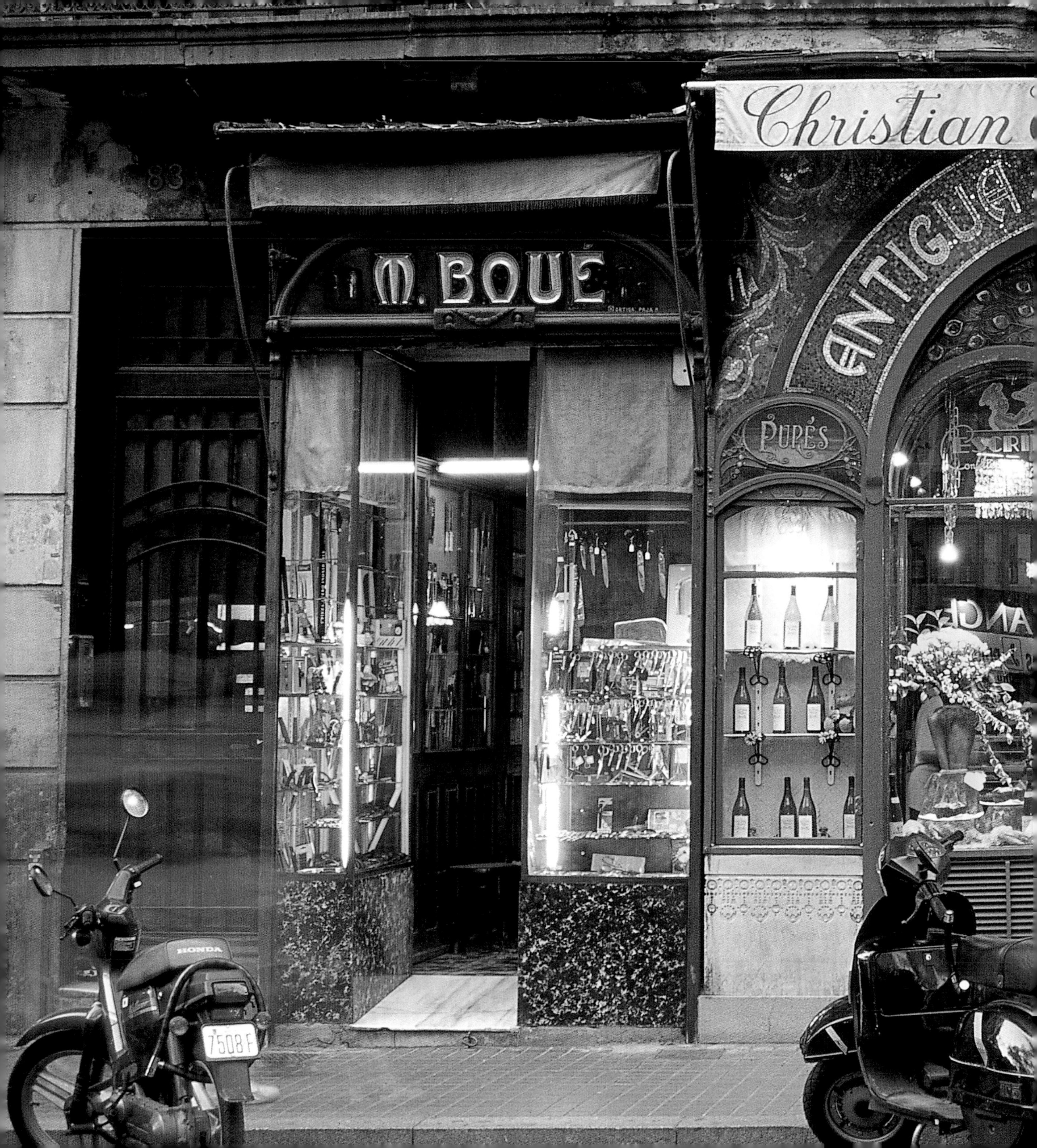

Christian
M. BOUE
ANTIGUA
PUPÉS
HONDA
7508 F

CONTENTS

INTRODUCTION

BEST OF BARCELONA

REFERENCE

RECIPES

INTRODUCTION

Situated on the Mediterranean coast, in the shadow of the Pyrenees, Barcelona is a bustling city with more than two thousand years of history. In the past two decades, it has reinvented itself as a vibrant cultural capital, making its mark in architecture, art, design, sports—and, of course, excellent food.

CULINARY HISTORY

Catalonia and its reigning city, Barcelona, have a long and fascinating culinary history, both with moments of glittering fame and long periods of obscurity. In fact, of all of Spain's regional cuisines, it may have the deepest historical roots. Like most southern European culinary traditions, from Provence to Turkey, Catalan cuisine has its origins in the great civilizations that once ruled the Mediterranean—most obviously the Romans, who brought the olive; the Greeks, who brought the grapevine; and the Arabs, who brought sugarcane, rice, and eggplant (aubergines). These raw materials flourished and are the basis of thriving industries today, including olive oil production and winemaking. When combined with the abundance of fish and shellfish from the Mediterranean and salt-cured hams and artisan cheeses from the Pyrenees, it is easy to see why Catalonia bears the marks of one of Europe's richest cuisines.

The first golden age of Catalan cuisine occurred in the Middle Ages. During the thirteenth and fourteenth centuries, the gastronomy of Catalonia and its capital,

Barcelona, was renowned across Europe. Classic Catalan dishes such as *menjar blanc* (almond-milk pudding) were often prepared at the courts of Naples and Rome, and in the mid-1400s, Italian food writer and historian Bartolomeo Sacchi (da Platina) declared Catalan cooks the best in the world.

Around the same time, some of the first food books printed in Europe were being written by Catalan authors, among them the famous *Llibre de Sent Sovi,* a collection of recipes likely produced near the end of the twelfth century. The *Regiment de Sanitat,* published in 1307, was a treatise on health and nutrition and contains a wealth of wisdom that is still true today, such as the suggestion to chew food slowly and calmly, to the accompaniment of "soft music." And finally, one of the greatest cookbooks of all time, *Llibre del Coch,* was first published in Barcelona around 1520. Written in Catalan by Ruperto de Nola, the cook to Spanish King Fernando I of Naples, this cookbook contains recipes drawn from Italian, Arabic, Provençal, and Catalan sources.

Even the two principal signifiers of Catalan food today come from the medieval era. One is the taste for exotic spices and for curious combinations of savory and sweet, as found in dishes like duck with pears and apples stuffed with meat. The other is the *picada,* a thickening agent made by pounding together nuts and herbs with a mortar and pestle. The resulting mixture is usually stirred into the recipe in its final cooking stage, contributing an added refinement to the flavor and texture of the finished dish.

Medieval Barcelona was famous not only for the quality of its cuisine but also for the quantity. Francesc Eiximenis (1327–1409), who taught in the great academic centers of medieval Europe, wrote, "[Barcelona] is gifted with great reason and peopled with notable folk of great weight and well nourished."

In the years following this age of splendor, however, Catalan cuisine fell into a gradual decline when the region was annexed by nearby Castile in the early eighteenth century. A period ensued in which the local culture was marginalized. Finally, in the early

nineteenth century, with the rise of a bourgeoisie and the incipient power of Barcelona as an economic and industrial capital, Catalonia began to assume some of its old importance. The year 1840 saw the publication of a guidebook to the city's inns and restaurants. (The famous Set Portes restaurant, located in Barcelona's waterfront neighborhood, Barceloneta, opened not long after and is still operating today.) During the latter part of the nineteenth century, Barcelona witnessed an influx of Italian restaurateurs, who influenced the cuisine and helped make pasta dishes like *canelons* (cannelloni) and *macarrons* (macaroni) regular items on many restaurant menus.

While the Spanish Civil War was also a bleak time for Catalonia, the postwar period was perhaps even more so. Nationalistic feeling was brutally suppressed, and the speaking, writing, and teaching of the Catalan language were prohibited. The culinary life of the region might have been richer, if there had been more food to go around. Many

Barcelonans have grim memories of the endless *escudella* (mixed meat and vegetable stew eaten with rice or pasta), the lack of culinary variety, the preponderance of salt cod, and the reliance on pork fat for frying.

With the arrival of democracy in the region in 1975 and the new freedoms that accompanied it, Catalan cooking underwent a revival. Josep Mercader, chef at the Hotel Empordà in Figueres, came to prominence by virtue of his elegant take on the traditional cooking of the region; his legacy lives on under the direction and able hands of his successor, Jaume Subirós. At the restaurant Big Rock, outside Platja d'Aro, Carles Camós began the work of rescuing traditional Catalan food from the doldrums into which it had sunk during the post–Civil War era. Inspired by these culinary revivalists, a roster of talented young chefs began to emerge, notably Santi Santamaria, Carme Ruscalleda, Carles Gaig, and Joan Roca. Traditional Catalan dishes were rediscovered and sometimes reinvented, while foreign flavors and new techniques were

incorporated as never before. Ferran Adrià and his restaurant El Bulli shot to fame (and to three Michelin stars) as the creator of a whole new attitude toward food and one of the most exciting chefs working anywhere in the world.

With Adrià at the helm, Catalan food is sailing into a second golden age. At the same time, care is being taken to avoid the loss of the traditional virtues of the cuisine in a swirl of foams and deconstructions. Pepa Aymamí and her Institut de la Cuina Catalana are working to ensure the survival of such classic Catalan dishes as *fricandó* (meat stew) and *rossejat* (rice or pasta baked in fish broth) in a world that has almost forgotten them. The institute is attempting to give Catalan cuisine protected status under UNESCO's World Heritage. Food writers such as Jaume Fàbrega and Pep Palau, as well as magazines like *Descobrir Cuina,* are also making vital contributions toward preserving the culinary legacy of the past.

They have their work cut out for them, because the region's food is continually evolving. In recent years, Barcelona has transformed itself into a multicultural capital, and the city's eating habits have changed along with it. Where once you could barely find a Chinese restaurant, now there are not only Chinese, but Indian, Moroccan, Mexican, Turkish, and Japanese ones as well. Even macrobiotic and vegetarian kitchens are popular. Indeed, the city's restaurant scene has never been so vibrant, and today Catalan cuisine is widely recognized as one of the most dynamic in the world.

CONTEMPORARY CUISINE

Barcelona's economy has boomed in the years since its triumphant hosting of the 1992 Olympics, and its food scene has blossomed along with it. Traditional cuisine is still the city's mainstay, but new trends and international influences are revitalizing the landscape, making Barcelona a culinary hot spot.

Defining Catalan cuisine is not easy. But then, defining Catalonia is not easy, either. It is a region with its own language and a strong sense of place and identity. At the same time, it is a part of the Spanish state, coexisting more or less harmoniously with Andalusia, Galicia, Navarre, and all of the other so-called autonomous communities that make up Spain.

The definition is further complicated by the *països catalans,* satellite regions of Catalan influence that sprang from the same historical roots, yet have no political connection with Catalonia itself. These "Catalan lands" consist of the region of Valencia, farther south down the coast of the Mediterranean; the Balearic Islands of Majorca, Minorca, Ibiza, and Formentera; an area known as French Catalonia, part of France extending north of the Spanish border; and the northwest corner of Sardinia in Italy.

As with geography, so with gastronomy. Catalonia is both separate from the rest of Spain and united to it by a great deal of commonality. In terms of cuisine, it is impossible to separate out a pure, unadulterated Catalan cuisine from the influences that surround it, hence the presence in this book of recipes for flan, gazpacho, and *croquetas.*

That said, it is the Catalans, perhaps along with the Basques, who possess the most sophisticated gastronomic life of any Spanish region. One factor is the sheer number of dishes that make up the repertoire of *la cuina catalana*—more than 150, according to some estimates. Another is the variety. Almost every *comarca* (county) of Catalonia, indeed almost every village, has something food-related that it claims as its own, whether it is a special vegetable variety, such as peas in the Maresme, turnips in the Empordà, and potatoes in Osona; a food-based fiesta like the *xatonada* of Sitges (see page 109); or a complex archaic dish like *El Niu,* from Palafrugell on the Costa Brava.

Catalans love their food and are serious about it, but not in a long-faced, solemn manner. *La cuina catalana* is food for families, for friends, and for communities. In its purest form, the cuisine of Catalonia is not naturally suited to the restaurant environment, and when it does appear on the menus of famous Catalan chefs like Santi Santamaria and Carme Ruscalleda, it is usually presented in a simplified and modernized form. It is essentially a rural and working-class tradition, the heritage of fishermen and peasant farmers.

But above all else, Catalan cooking is Mediterranean. The presence of the sea is probably the single most important influence on the way people eat in this part of the world. Catalonia has more than two hundred miles (325 km) of coastline, so it comes as no surprise that fish and shellfish are pillars of the local diet. Fresh fish is normally grilled (the favorite cooking technique), baked, or combined with potatoes and stock in an *all cremat, suquet, romesco, sarsuela,* or one of the dozen or so other Catalan variants of fish

stew. Shrimp (prawns) and other crustaceans are of superb quality, particularly the famous *gambes de Palamós.* Cured and preserved fish plays an important role: The salted anchovies of the coastal town L'Escala are famous throughout Spain. Salt cod is also extremely popular and forms the basis for some of Catalonia's most famous dishes, notably *xató* (escarole salad with salt cod; page 109), *esqueixada* (shredded salt cod salad; page 36), and *bacallà a la llauna* (oven-roasted salt cod with garlic and pimentón).

Gastronomically (and geographically) speaking, the region is divided according to a powerful logic, with rivers, fertile plains, deserts, and soaring mountains. From the inland zones come fine meats and dairy products, fruits and vegetables, and snails. From the mountains come game, and trout from the Pyrenean rivers. Rice from the Ebro Delta in the south of the region is used in dishes like *arròs negre* (black rice), *arròs a banda* (rice with fish stock), and various local versions of paella.

Any world cuisine worthy of consideration gives the greatest respect to vegetables, and *la cuina catalana* is no exception. The sensational displays at markets such as Barcelona's La Boqueria are powerful evidence that the quality is high. Some of the best Catalan dishes are based on vegetables: fava (broad) beans for *faves a la catalana* (page 113), spinach with raisins and pine nuts, and cabbage and potatoes for *trinxat* (page 114). Wild mushrooms are a national obsession, and the forests teem with mushroom hunters during the autumn months. Dried pulses, such as lentils, beans, and chickpeas (garbanzos), form the basis for rib-sticking soup-stews like the famous *escudella i carn d'olla* (page 153).

Despite the variety in Catalan cuisine, there are some generalizations that can be made. Catalan eaters by and large seem to enjoy the mixture of sweet and sour more than any other people in Western Europe— arguably a legacy of the medieval glory days of *la cuina catalana.* (A propensity for adding

spices, particularly cinnamon, to meat dishes is surely a medieval throwback, too.) They adore the flavor and texture of nuts, which are pounded with herbs as part of the famous *picada* and used as a thickener for braised and baked dishes. They have a notable sweet tooth, so a good *pastisseria,* or pastry shop, in Catalonia will never be short of clientele.

Both Catalans and their food are by nature festive and celebratory. Any excuse will do to throw a party based around one of their favorite dishes, whether it be the *truita amb suc,* a spinach omelet with tomato sauce (page 126) from the Priorat, or the *cassola de tros,* a monumental stew of rabbit, snails, and mixed vegetables, each of which has its corresponding *festa.* Taking part in *la*

calçotada, the feast of a special type of grilled green (spring) onions called *calçots,* dunked in *romesco* sauce, is an intensely Catalan experience in itself (see page 121).

And at the heart of it all, where the various crosscurrents of Catalan cuisine meet and mingle, is the city of Barcelona. If the Catalan capital has not historically been famous for food, it is perhaps only because Gaudí, the Olympics, the Barcelona football club, and the reputation of the city as a world design mecca have stolen its thunder as a gastronomic capital. The situation is rapidly changing, however, as culinary observers worldwide realize that, both in terms of traditional and contemporary cooking, Barcelona represents a formidable force.

DINING OUT

Until recently, Barcelona was a city where meals were often eaten at home and cooked in a traditional style. Nowadays, the reverse is true. This is a city in love with eating out. Restaurants of all types, sizes, and price levels abound in every neighborhood, and if variety is the spice of life, Barcelona is a hot prospect indeed.

In a part of the world where life, or much of its social activity, plays out *al carrer*—"in the street"—the restaurant forms a vitally important part of the local culture. It is seen as a neutral space, free from the tedious routines of home and work, where the only imperatives are sensuous enjoyment and the pleasure of human interaction.

As a restaurant town, Barcelona may not be on the A list with Paris or New York, but it is certainly riding at the top of the B list. The choice and variety are enormous, and it is

possible to eat well on any budget. At the lower end of the price scale are the *casas de comida,* simple eating houses where a full three-course meal, including wine and coffee, can be had for very little money. At the upper end of the scale, the wizardlike chefs of Barcelona cuisine work their magic for those who can afford it at grand restaurants like Neichel, Jean Luc Figueras, Gaig, Drolma, and Talaia-Mar.

In between these extremes are the neighborhood restaurants, the chic, so-called

restaurants de disseny, where the style of the place has as much to say as the food on your plate: the fish restaurants, the *asadores* (grill rooms), and the beachside *chiringuitos*. Then there are the ethnic restaurants, a sector that has blossomed marvelously in recent years, with the foods of Japan, China, Pakistan, Turkey, Lebanon, and Morocco all well represented. Also prominent are restaurants serving dishes from other regions of Spain, notably Galicia, Andalusia, and the Basque country, fare from closer to home but still vaguely exotic, even to locals.

Ironically, although foreign and fusion cuisines fill the culinary limelight—testimony to Barcelona's openmindedness—authentic Catalan cooking, the kind of food the region's grandmothers used to make, seems underrepresented in Barcelona. Luckily, the city has a handful of restaurants that have always served real Catalan food and show no signs of letting it fade into the shadows. Set Portes, founded in 1836 and still serving *paella Parellada* (rice with seafood and mixed

meats; page 137) and *canelons de festa* (baked cannelloni; page 129) to appreciative hordes of tourists and locals alike, is the most famous of the lot. Another local favorite is Gargantua i Pantagruel, a sleekly designed restaurant majoring in the specialties of Lleida and the surrounding region—dishes like *cargols a la llauna* (baked snails) and *bacallà* (salt cod) with honey. Estimable traditional preparations are featured at Senyor Parellada, the flagship of Ramón Parellada's small chain of restored lodging houses. Cal Isidre, run for two decades by Isidre Gironés, his wife Montse, and daughter Núria, is a restaurant that understands perhaps best of all how to coax the glories of classic Catalan cuisine into the modern world. This is one of the few eateries in Barcelona where one can enjoy a perfectly presented *bacallà a la llauna* (oven-roasted salt cod) or a scrumptious *suquet* (stew) of monkfish.

Three of the longest-running *casas de comida* in town are Cal Estevet, Can Lluis, and Can Culleretes (the last was founded in

1740, making it one of the oldest restaurants in the world), all serving hearty meals with wine at modest prices. El Celler Nou represents a slightly more upmarket option, though it is thoroughly Catalan in its tavernlike decoration and appealingly rustic cooking.

For a taste of the classic Spanish *chiringuito*, the kind of beachside restaurant where you shake off the sand from your feet as you come through the door, try the family-run Xiringuito Escribà on Bogatell beach (just south of the Olympic village) owned by the Escribà brothers (see Pastisseries, page 65). With a menu devised by Carles Abellán of the upscale Comerç 24 and desserts from the Escribà family, the food is a cut above the average *chiringuito*, and there is nowhere better in Barcelona to see, smell, and hear the sea as you feast on local seafood.

Away from the city's sometimes frenzied jostling for fashionability, both food and life tend to stick closer to the land. Out in the Catalan countryside, a new generation is looking again at its culinary roots while

smoothly assimilating the influence of modernist fashions. In the hills around the town of Vic, a collective of young chefs calling itself Osona Cuina is doing a great job of promoting the range of local ingredients, including wild mushrooms and truffles, potatoes, and game. The collective, along with other individuals in Vic, such as Nando Jubany and Jordi Parramón, is today's equivalent of the generation of farsighted chefs who revolutionized Catalan cooking in the 1980s. Further off the beaten path in Catalonia, in a town called Olot, another champion of the new Spanish cuisine has found itself in Les Cols, a restaurant that practically brings the farmyard to the table.

The work of the new Catalan chefs in Barcelona encompasses a wide range of different styles, from the sophisticated luxury of Xavier Pellicer at Abac and Fermi Puig at Drolma to the streetwise swagger of places like Ot, Hisop, Sauc, and Biblioteca. The last few years have seen a mania for fusion food, mixing and matching Asian ingredients with

Mediterranean techniques (or the other way around). Although this tendency is fast approaching the saturation point, there is still excitement to be found in the trendy, design-driven restaurants of neighborhoods like the Born and Raval. Today, the DJ restaurant, in which a person in headphones spins dance music while you try to make yourself heard across the table, is very much in vogue in Barcelona (Salsitas, Oven, Salero, and Fuse are good examples), as are restaurants conceived as lounges, where diners can linger into the early hours.

While women may have long been the stalwarts of Catalan home cooking, the star chefs of haute cuisine have been men. At last, however, women's contributions to the culinary scene are being recognized, and some of the most important chefs in Catalonia are female. Paquita and Lolita Reixach, who began running a truckstop fifty years ago, are now acclaimed for their magnificent rustic cooking at one of the country's best restaurants, the Hispania in Arenys de Mar.

A little farther along the coast, in Sant Pol de Mar, is another culinary wizard, Carme Ruscalleda, perhaps the most brilliant of all Catalonia's cooks, male or female, and certainly among the world's outstanding women chefs. Ruscalleda is a culinary powerhouse whose capacity for work is as unlimited as her imagination. Her cooking might be described as a contemporary and intensely personal take on the Catalan food of her childhood, a reflection of the rich trove of local products that ranges from fish and shellfish to vegetables and fruit.

As you might expect from a community with a long Mediterranean coastline, Catalonia has an enormous appetite for the local catch. Seafood restaurants form a vital and important category within the food scene, especially in the towns and cities of the Mediterranean seaboard. In Barcelona itself, fish cooking in general is of high quality, but it is truly exceptional in the Barceloneta, a one-time fishing district just below the Barri Gòtic. The harbor front of the Port Vell (old port) is a long

strip of restaurants, nearly all of which specialize in *la cuina marinera*—"seafood cooking." The typical menu in this part of town centers around fish *a la planxa* (seared on a griddle; *a la placha* in Spanish) or as part of a mixed rice dish like *arròs a banda* (cooked with fish stock) and paella or of the pasta-based *fideuà*. Certain dishes at El Suquet de l'Almirall are famed throughout Barcelona: the crisp *calamares a la romana* (line-caught squid battered and fried in olive oil), for example, are reputed to be the best in the city. Els Pescadors, in the city's once little-visited, but increasingly popular Poble Nou district, is a long-running operation that hits all the right notes: a lovely old dining room with its original whitewashed walls and marble tables and a menu that goes beyond the usual seafood repertoire into *fricandó de rap* (monkfish stew) and *arròs cremós de gambes amb formatge fumat* (creamy rice with shrimp and smoked goat cheese).

MARKETS

All over the world, supermarkets are replacing traditional food markets, which are quickly becoming a thing of the past. Not so in Barcelona. The city's neighborhood markets are very much alive, and none more so than the bustling Mercat de Sant Josep, known as La Boqueria, one of best places to shop for seasonal foods.

People visiting Barcelona for the first time are often surprised to discover that, along with the renowned Gaudí buildings and the Picasso Museum, the city also possesses one of the world's greatest food markets. The Mercat de Sant Josep, better known as La Boqueria, is one of about forty covered food markets in the capital, and the most spectacular. Others worth a look are the Mercat de Sant Antoni, with its grand Parisian-style ironwork building, and the charming Mercat de Gràcia, in the Gràcia neighborhood. Oddly, Barcelona does not have many open-air food markets, though there is one notable exception: the Plaça del Pi. Held on the first Saturday and Sunday of every month, this market offers artisan cheeses, chocolate, herbs, honey, baked goods, and other locally made products.

La Boqueria was once the site of a convent of Carmelite monks, until the structure burned down in 1835 and a fine new market was established in its place. In 1914, it was given a roof and a decorative stained-glass *modernista* entrance where it leads directly off the Ramblas, Barcelona's bustling main promenade. It is a cause for celebration that this huge and vibrant market—the largest in Spain at about twenty thousand square feet (6,000 sq m)—is still alive and kicking at the heart of the city center and hasn't been hauled out to the suburbs to make way for ritzy shops and apartments. For the three hundred families who make their living here, La Boqueria is just like a village, complete with gossip, friendships, and village personalities, such as Juanito at the Bar

Pinotxo, fruiterer Eduard Soley, and Marta at the fish stall Peixos Marta.

La Boqueria represents all that is best in Catalan ingredients (though not always at the best possible prices). Most of the top-quality local produce finds its way to this market. In the fish section, the booth Marisc Genaro is especially worth a visit for its displays of shellfish. Salted and cured fish, such as *bacallà,* cured tuna roe, and salted herrings are the order of the day at Especialitats Salaons. No less than seventy-two fruit and vegetable stalls cover the entire range of Catalan and Spanish produce, and exotic fruits, even such eccentricities as starfruit and durian, are increasingly easy to find, too. For hams and charcuterie, the best source is generally thought to be Cansaladeria Mateo López, where maestro Mateo specializes in Iberian hams and other fine pork products, many from beyond the borders of Catalonia, excellent in their own right.

All tastes are catered to at La Boqueria. If it's snails you want, the place to go is a tiny, nameless stall on the corner of the Carrer Sagres. A scrawled notice advertises *auténtics cargols de Lleida*—"genuine snails from the town of Lleida"—in sizes ranging from big, fat Vinyals to the smaller Monxeta and Bobe varieties. If your taste runs to game meats, Salvador Capdevila will sell you just about anything your heart desires, from venison, boar, and hare to partridge and duck.

The bars of La Boqueria are a vital element of the market's broader function. Hearty *esmorzars de forquilla* (simply prepared "fork" breakfasts) featuring such dishes as braised pig's feet and salt cod with beans are served up for the market workers at a time of the morning when most of us are just beginning to contemplate our first cup of coffee. The Bar Pinotxo, near the entrance, is perhaps the market's most famous tapas bar and its owner, Juanito, its best-known personality. While he presides out front, chatting with customers, preparing coffee, or pouring drinks, the younger generation cooks up dozens of orders at the back of the tiny kitchen, making good use of the day's freshest produce. Among other delights, Bar Pinotxo makes one of the finest *pa amb tomàquet* (tomato-rubbed bread; page 75) in Barcelona. El Quim de la Boqueria in the heart of the market is a nice place to take the weight off your feet and try a little tapa, a medium-sized *ración,* a *bocadillo* (sandwich), or a full-scale meal. Proprietor Quim is busy at the stove beginning at eight in the morning, then later he composes a brilliant menu reflecting his morning's adventures around the stalls. Never has "market cooking" been more exactly that.

Before you leave, don't miss the simple stalls set up outside the market by women who bring in their produce from the *masies* (rural farmhouses). These stalls aren't officially part of the market, for their owners operate on a smaller, less ambitious scale, but the quality is just as high. Here you will often see Pakistani and Moroccan immigrants doing their shopping. Clearly they know a good thing when they see it—as do all the clients of the beautiful La Boqueria.

FLAVORS OF BARCELONA AND CATALONIA

Eating in Barcelona is a complex interplay of origins, influences, and traditions. As you travel through the city's neighborhoods, keep your eyes open and your palate attuned to the different flavors offered at each stop. The same is true in the surrounding regions, where the cuisines are united by a common history.

Barri Gòtic

Some of Barcelona's prime food hot spots are found in the the tourist-ridden streets of the medieval old town known as Barri Gòtic. The dominant categories here are old-fashioned Catalan restaurants with historical roots—places like Can Culleretes (established in 1740) and Agut (established in 1924)—and ancient taverns perfect for a glass of wine and a bite to eat. Look for the superlative Els Quatre Gats, El Xampanyet, or El Pintor. Formatgeria La Seu, a shop specializing in Spanish farmhouse cheeses, is a gem, and around the corner, El Mesón del Café serves perhaps Barcelona's best cup of coffee. Shunka, close to the cathedral, is a superb Japanese restaurant frequented by the likes of renowned chef Ferran Adrià.

Born

Clustered around the former produce market of Born, this neighborhood (the southern end of which is known as La Ribera), is Barcelona's fashion zone. It is also the heartland of trendy restaurants patronized by trendy people, featuring chefs creating wild fusion cuisine with an emphasis on Asian flavors. Visit Nao Colon, Salero, Arrel del Born, or Café Kafka for some of the best experiences of this kind.

Amid the designer frippery characterizing this neighborhood is some real creative excellence: Check out the inventive tapas at Santa Maria, Estrella de Plata, Cal Pep, or

Comerç 24, Carles Abellán's highly fashionable postmodern tapas salon. La Vinya del Senyor is one of the city's best wine bars, and Abac is possibly its finest restaurant.

Raval

Raval is a melting pot of immigrants from Africa, Asia, South America, and eastern Europe. Once the Barrio Chino, or Chinatown, this neighborhood now hums with Asian supermarkets, halal butchers, and designer delis—not to mention La Boqueria market (page 25). Predominant flavors are spicy and exotic, reflecting the influx of Pakistanis and Moroccans into the barrio. The Shalimar on Carrer Carme was Barcelona's first Pakistani restaurant and still ranks as one of the best. Meanwhile, the bohemian invasion of Raval has spawned a new wave of designer "lounges" combining electronic music with chic design and audacious fusion food.

Barceloneta

As befits this former fishing district down by the sea, the Barceloneta is a great destination for seafood. Fish lovers prowl the narrow streets of this wonderfully atmospheric barrio in search of classic fish stews like *suquet* and *sarsuela,* as well as other Catalan fish dishes. Start off with tapas at Cova Fumada, then move on to Cheriff, reputed to serve Barcelona's best paella, or to Restaurant Barceloneta for *arròs negre* (black rice) and

staggering plates of shellfish. Can Majó, run by the Suárez family for the last thirty years, is reliably high quality and has a lovely open-air *terraza.* The famous seafood restaurant Can Solé still has its original one-hundred-year-old decor. Ricart, the fish shop just around the corner, was founded in 1939.

L'Eixample

L'Eixample is the nerve center of bourgeois Barcelona. Passeig de Gràcia, a lively avenue cutting through the neighborhood, is where you will find three famous, elaborate buildings by architect Antoni Gaudí. L'Eixample is also home to a many of the city's grandest restaurants. Hotel restaurants come into their own here: at the top are Drolma in the Hotel Majestic and East 47 at Hotel Claris. This high-end neighborhood tends toward a more progressive take on contemporary cuisine; Sauc and Hisop are two restaurants to watch for new trends. Keep an eye out for old *colmados,* or general stores, that are now enjoying a new lease on life as luxury delis.

The best include Mantequeria Ravell, Murrià, and Quílez, with superb selections of local cheeses, cured meats, and sausages and an excellent selection of wines. Finally, be sure to visit the barrio's two state-of-the-art chocolate makers, Xocoa and Sampaka.

Gràcia

This former working-class district has a quiet bohemian charm and some intriguing food offerings. Lebanese, Turkish, Greek, and Balkan foods are conspicuous; there are few better places in Barcelona to get a good souvlaki. Another culinary treat is the barrio's ethnic pastries, which range from bagels to Argentinian empanadas to the unusual Arab pastries at Principe. The bread at Fleca Fortino rates among the best in Barcelona. Mercat de Llibertat, housed in a charming, art nouveau ironwork building, functions as the neighborhood food market but is better than central markets you find in most cities. The neighborhood is also home to Ot, one of Barcelona's most exciting new restaurants.

Girona, Empordà, and Costa Brava

This northern coastal area of Catalonia has a unique gastronomic tradition of its own: *mar i muntanya,* the mixing of seafood with meat. The *platillos* of the Empordà are rich, rustic combinations of organ meats, snails, and game. At its best, the fish and seafood of the Costa Brava are peerless. The *suquet,* a simple Catalan stew of fish and potatoes is superb, and don't miss the famed shrimp from the coastal towns of Palamós and Roses. Some of the best restaurants in Catalonia are found in this region. The kitchen at Hotel Empordà was one of the progenitors of the new Catalan cuisine and is still going strong under chef Jaume Subirós. In Girona, you will find Celler de Can Roca, one of the very best restaurants in Spain, and farther up the Costa Brava, in the town of Roses, is a local restaurant known around the world: El Bulli.

Lleida

Lleida is one of Spain's great fruit-growing regions. The apples, pears, and plums are

famous, as are the vegetables grown on the well-watered plains around it. Les Garrigues, an important olive oil–producing region in Llieda, makes a golden yellow, fruity oil of superb quality. Catalan cuisine also relies on another major product of this area: almonds, pistachios, and other nuts. The southern part of this region has a huge appetite for snails, which are typically cooked *a la llauna* ("on the tin," roasted in the oven) or *a la gormanda* (with onion, ham, garlic, and chiles). Aplec del Cargol is Lleida's great festival for snail lovers. The northern part of Lleida takes in the high Pyrenees, with distinct culinary contributions, such as fine goat's and sheep's milk cheeses and French-influenced dishes like *sopa de ceba* (onion soup).

Tarragona

Tarragona constitutes the southernmost part of Catalonia proper, halfway between Barcelona and the Catalan-speaking lands of Valencia and Alicante. The town of Valls, and by extension the whole region, is best known gastronomically for its massive consumption of *calçots* (grilled green onions; page 121). Tarragona is also the home of *romesco*—the fish stew and the sauce of the same name, both of which feature ground nuts—and of the salad *xató*. Rice from the Ebro Delta is produced in small quantities, but it is of exceptional quality. Honey from the fragrant hills of Port de Beseit is said to be the best in Catalonia. Inland is the mountainous zone where some of Spain's finest red wines are made. Monsant, Priorat, and Tarragona are three highly respected local growing areas.

Països Catalans

The *països catalans* extend beyond the official boundaries of Catalonia and include the "autonomous community" of Valencia, the four Balearic islands (Majorca, Minorca, Ibiza, and Formentera), the Pyrenean enclave of Andorra, and the northwest corner of Sardinia.

Valencia is synonymous with one of the best-loved dishes in the Spanish repertoire, *paella valenciana*. In fact, rice is the basis for many Valencian dishes, including *arròs a banda* (rice with fish stock), *arròs al forn* (baked rice), and the famous *arròs amb crosta* of Elche (baked rice with an egg crust; page 145). Valencia is also known for its bounty of fresh fruits and vegetables—the region is Europe's leading producer of oranges—and the city's beautiful Mercat Central is second only to Barcelona's La Boqueria in size and excellence. From the southern part of the region, whose capital is Alicante, come the fabulous *turrons* (almond nougats), enjoyed at Christmas all over Spain.

The Balearic Islands are collectively a rich source of good things to eat. The four islands of this archipelago share many ingredients and dishes, but equally, each island is fiercely proud of its own culinary tradition. Seafood naturally forms a major part of the island diet, followed by the products of the *matanza—sobrassada,* a minced raw pork sausage cured with pimentón, is a Balearic specialty. Vegetables, fruit, and nuts, especially almonds, also play an important role.

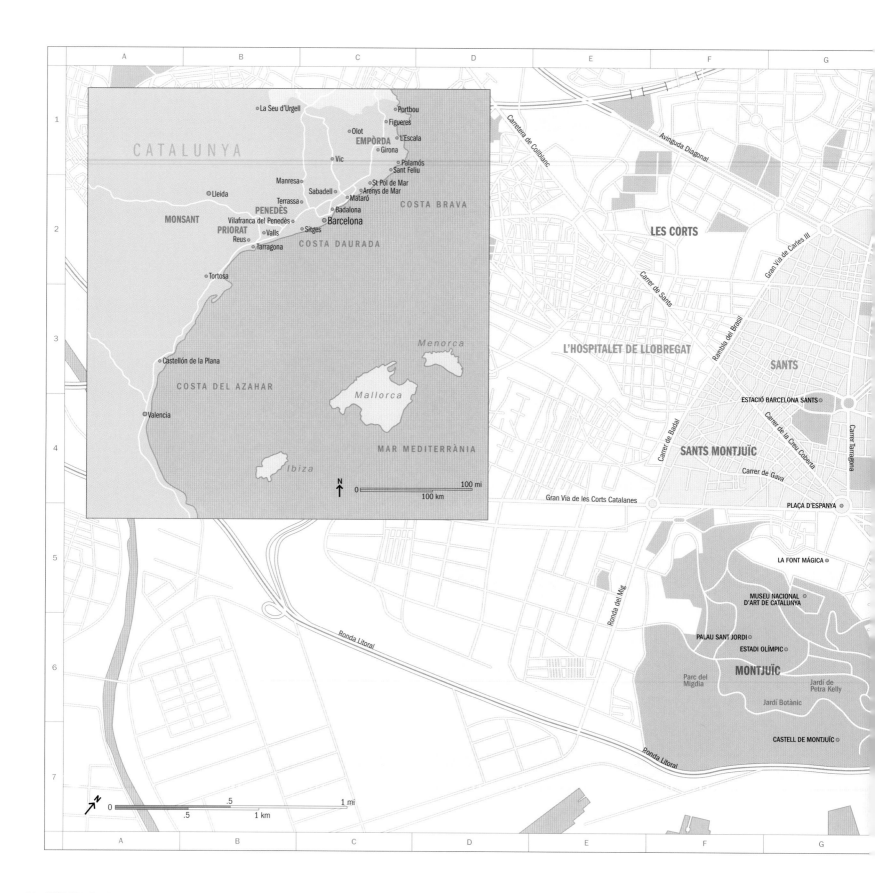

La Seu d'Urgell
Portbou
Figueres
Olot
L'Escala
EMPÒRDA
CATALUNYA
Vic
Girona
Palamós
Sant Feliu
Manresa
St Pol de Mar
Lleida
Sabadell
Arenys de Mar
Terrassa
Mataró
COSTA BRAVA
MONSANT
PENEDÈS
Badalona
PRIORAT
Vilafranca del Penedès
Barcelona
Reus
Valls
Sitges
COSTA DAURADA
Tarragona

Tortosa

Menorca

Castellón de la Plana

COSTA DEL AZAHAR
Mallorca

Valencia

MAR MEDITERRÀNIA

Ibiza

N
0   100 mi
0   100 km

Carretera de Collblanc
Avinguda Diagonal

LES CORTS
Gran Via de Carles III

Carrer de Sants

L'HOSPITALET DE LLOBREGAT
Rambla del Brasil
SANTS

ESTACIÓ BARCELONA SANTS

Carrer de la Creu Coberta
Carrer de Badal
Carrer Tarragona
Carrer de Gava
SANTS MONTJUÏC

PLAÇA D'ESPANYA
Gran Via de les Corts Catalanes

LA FONT MÀGICA

Ronda del Mig

MUSEU NACIONAL
D'ART DE CATALUNYA

Ronda Litoral

PALAU SANT JORDI

ESTADI OLÍMPIC

MONTJUÏC
Parc del
Migdia
Jardí de
Petra Kelly

Jardí Botànic

Ronda Litoral

CASTELL DE MONTJUÏC

N
0   .5   1 mi
0   .5   1 km

SARRIÀ·SANT GERVASI

Parc la Creueta del Coll

Jardins del Turó del Putget

Ronda del General Mitre

Parc Güell

HORTA

L'EIXAMPLE

SANTS

SAGRADA FAMILIA ⊚

Area of Culinary Interest

Parks

Culinary Neighborhoods

Neighborhoods

Point of Interest

EL CARMEL

VILAPICINA

Via Augusta

Jardins del Poeta Eduard Marquina

Travessera de Dalt

Parc del Guinardó

GRÀCIA

EL GUINARDÓ

Parc de les Aigües

CONGRES

Ronda del Guinardó

Parc Pégaso

Carrer del Comte d'Urgell

B A R C E L O N A

Avinguda de Gaudí

CAMP DE L'ARPA

Avinguda Meridiana

SANT MARTÍ DE PROVENÇALS

Passeig de Sant Joan

Avinguda Diagonal

Passeig de Gràcia

⊚ LA PEDRERA

⊚ SAGRADA FAMILIA

Parc de Sant Martí

Avinguda de Roma

L'EIXAMPLE

Carrer D'Aragó

LA DRETA DE L'EIXAMPLE

EL CLOT

Carrer d'Aragó

LA VERNEDA

CASA BATLLÓ ⊚

UNIVERSITAT CENTRAL ⊚

⊚ CASA AMATLLER

PLAÇA DE TETUAN ⊚

⊚ PLAÇA DE TOROS

Parc de Clot

Gran Via de les Corts Catalanes

Gran Via de les Corts Catalanes

SANT ANTONI

Avinguda Mistral

Ronda de Sant Antoni

⊚ MACBA

⊚ PLAÇA DE CATALUNYA

Ronda de Sant Pere

Via Laietana

PLAÇA DE LES GLÒRIES CATALANES

Avinguda Diagonal

SANT MARTÍ

⊚ MERCAT DE SANT ANTONI

Ronda de Sant Pau

RAVAL

ARC DE TRIOMF ⊚

Parc Estació del Nord

Avinguda Meridiana

EL POBLE NOU

Carrer de Pere IV

⊚ MERCAT DE LA BOQUERIA

Avinguda del Paral·lel

La Rambla

⊚ CATEDRAL

GRAN TEATRE DEL LICEU ⊚

BARRI GÒTIC

⊚ MUSEU PICASSO

Parc de la Ciutadella

Jardins de Mercè Plantada

POBLE SEC

BORN

MERCAT DEL BORN ⊚

⊚ MUSEU D'ART MODERN

PORT VELL

CIUTAT VELLA

Passeig Isabel II

Passeig de Colóm

⊚ ESTACIÓ DE FRANÇA

⊚ MUSEU MARÍTIM

COLÓM ⊚

Parc Zoológic Acuarama

Avinguda D'Icària

Parc del Port Olímpic

Parc Diagonal Mar

PLAÇA DE LES DRASSANES

Ronda Litoral

VILA OLÍMPIC

Parc del Poblenou

⊚ PORT BARCELONA

⊚ BEACH BOGATELL

⊚ PORT VELL

BARCELONETA

⊚ PORT OLÍMPIC

⊚ BARCELONETA BEACH

MAR MEDITERRÀNIA

Best of **BARCELONA**

Whatever venue you choose for taking an aperitif in Barcelona, you will find something there to eat with it: a plate of *ibérico* ham, a slice of Manchego cheese, toasted bread rubbed with tomato and drizzled with olive oil *(pa amb tomàquet)*, a bowl of spicy olives.

TAPAS

Catalonia has a complex relationship with the rest of Spain, and this is as true of its eating—and snacking—habits as anything else. A wide variety of tapas, little dishes served with drinks, are served all over Spain, including Catalonia. But the tapas habit still belongs more to the non-Catalans in Catalonia than to the Catalans themselves. When the locals snack, they do it differently. *Raciones* (medium-sized servings) of sliced sausage and hams; *entrepans* stuffed with fresh cheese and anchovies (page 79); bowls of olives and nuts; or tomato-rubbed bread (page 75) are local alternatives to the typical Spanish repertoire of tapas. That said, you can find excellent tapas in Barcelona. Cal Pep and Bar Pinotxo (in La Boqueria market) are arguably the two best tapas outposts in town and are deservedly popular with locals.

Other Spanish regional traditions have made their mark on Catalan eating habits as well. Basque-style bars have cropped up around Barcelona, with trays of *pintxos* (snacks) on the bar to be eaten at will and paid for later. The favorite drinks are dry red Rioja wine or cider, served in the flat-bottomed glasses typical of the Basque country. Galicians were probably the first immigrants to establish a community in Barcelona, and many of their bars offer such regional small dishes as *pulpo a feira* (octopus with paprika and olive oil) or tuna-stuffed empanadas. Meanwhile, updated *cerveserias*—stylish "beer halls" like the Ciudad Condal—cheerfully mix and match local food and drink traditions with whatever takes their fancy.

Some of the best tapas in town are tangy snacks composed of cured or pickled foods.

At Quimet i Quimet, a one-room bodega in Poble Sec, the selection, or *surtido,* is a miniature feast made up daily on the spot from such items as wild mushrooms in oil, tuna *escabetx,* pickled baby onions, or slices of *mojama* (cured tuna roe). Xampanyet, a few doors down from the Picasso Museum, also majors in pickled delectables—don't miss the crunchy, sweet whole garlic cloves.

Finally, the newest wave in snacking is called the *tapa de autor.* Chefs like Carles Abellán, at superchic Comerç 24; Paco Guzmán, presiding at Santa Maria across the street; and Didac López, of Estrella de Plata, delight in creating miniature dishes reflecting their interest in fusion food and contemporary trends. Elegant nibbles like duck liver with hibiscus-flower syrup or tuna sashimi pizza are causing great excitement in Barcelona.

Spanish regional traditions have made their mark on Catalan eating habits.

BOQUERONES EN VINAGRE

CALAMARS A LA ROMANA

ESQUEIXADA DE BACALLÀ

PATATAS BRAVAS

BOQUERONES EN VINAGRE

The origins of this delicious tapa are uncertain, but it is now found all over Spain. Fresh anchovies are filleted, cured in vinegar and salt, and dressed with olive oil, minced garlic, and parsley. The tangy vinegar marinade makes these little fish a perfect foil for a glass of cold Manzanilla or other fine dry sherry. Look for *boquerones* with firm white flesh, an indication of quality.

ESQUEIXADA DE BACALLÀ

Well-loved main courses featuring *bacallà,* or salt cod, abound throughout Catalonia, and this popular salad is an adaptation of these classic dishes. Strips of salt cod (the verb *esqueixar* means "to shred") are tossed with roasted red peppers, onions, tomatoes, and black olives. The resulting taste experience is a fine invention indeed: the saltiness of the cod is perfectly balanced by the sweetness of the bell peppers (capsicums). It is delicious paired with a glass of dry white wine.

CALAMARS A LA ROMANA

"Roman-style" squid rings are a timeless classic of Spanish bar-top snacking. But there are *calamars* and then there are *calamars.* Unscrupulous places cook up frozen precooked squid, but honest establishments use only the fresh seafood, sliced, battered, and fried to sizzling crispness in olive oil. These light, crisp, and tender morsels are typically served with a sprinkling of salt and a wedge of lemon. For the perfect match, accompany them with a glass of beer or a jug of sangria.

PATATAS BRAVAS

Deep-fried potato chunks served with a spicy sauce, *patatas bravas* are a favorite snack food with students and young people, probably because they're both inexpensive and tasty. This satisfying dish is also a midday favorite with working people who often wash it down with a glass of red wine. Originally hailing from Madrid, *patatas bravas* (the name means "brave potatoes") are now found in most Barcelona tapas bars.

CARGOLS

PERNIL IBÉRIC
(JAMÓN IBÉRICO)

CROQUETAS

BERBERECHOS

CARGOLS

To the Catalan gourmet, a bowlful of fresh snails is a thing of beauty. *Cargols* (*caracoles* in Spanish) are usually roasted *a la llauna* (in a special tin pan) or cooked in a simple sauce with garlic, red bell pepper (capsicum), and perhaps a little blood sausage and a hint of chile. To extract the snail from its shell, insert a tiny snail fork, the tip of a small knife, or a wooden toothpick as far inside the shell as you can and twist.

CROQUETAS

These golden brown croquettes originated as a tasty way to use up leftovers from the Sunday *carn d'olla* (meat stew), but they have become a classic snack food favored all over Spain. They have a crispy crumb coating and are meltingly tender on the inside. *Croquetas* are most commonly made with ham or chicken or a combination, although inventive fillings based on ingredients like wild mushrooms, shrimp, and spinach are starting to appear at some of the more forward-looking tapas bars in the city.

PERNIL IBÉRIC
(JAMÓN IBÉRICO)

Cured ham from the Iberian pig is not made in Catalonia. It hails instead from the western regions of Andalusia and Extremadura, where the pigs roam the forests in a semiwild state, feeding on acorns. But a product as good as this one was bound to be popular in Barcelona. *Pernil ibéric* is served in small slices cut directly from the ham at the moment of ordering. It makes a delicious tapa with beer or a glass of good red wine or *cava* (page 56).

BERBERECHOS

These tiny clams, almost always canned in their own juices, are a traditional accompaniment to the midday glass of vermouth. *Berberechos* are farmed in huge quantities in the estuaries off the western coast of Spain in Galicia, where they are fished by women known as *marisqueiras*. They are usually eaten by sprinkling them with a squeeze of lemon, then spearing them with a toothpick.

The love of pork in all its forms is a touchstone for the people of the Iberian peninsula that dates back centuries, to when its enthusiastic consumption was almost an article of faith. The *matanza,* or pig slaughter, is still celebrated once a year in rural homes, and the products resulting from it are as popular as ever.

XARCUTERIA

The love of meat, in particular ham and sausages, reaches near cult status in Spain. Nowhere is it better displayed than in Barcelona's highly trafficked *xarcuterias,* which are stocked with *pernils salats* (salt-cured hams) from the Pyrenees, *cansalada* (cured pork fat), a multitude of *embotits* (sausages), and other culinary treasures.

There are two basic types of sausage, cured and fresh. The latter is made up principally by various kinds of *botifarra:* fat pork sausages meant to be grilled and served with beans, a dish known as *mongetes amb botifarra;* or preboiled sausages, including *botifarra blanca, botifarra negra* (blood sausage), and *botifarra catalana* (made with truffles and sweet wine). Among cured sausages, the most famous is *salchichón,* also called *llonganissa.* The headquarters of

salchichón production is the town of Vic, which has a perfect climate for sausage curing—cold, dry, and misty—and a proud tradition stretching back at least two hundred years. The standard-bearer for *salchichón* quality in Vic is the house of Casa Sendra, founded in 1849 and still in operation. Casa Sendra follows an artisanal process, using the best parts of the pig and curing them for five to nine months. The result is a meaty, firm-textured, and flavorful slicing sausage.

Other Catalan pork specialties include *baldana de arròs* from the town of Tortosa, made with rice and a variety of nuts; and *pa de fetge,* a country pâté from the Cerdanya (page 83). The notoriously sweet *botifarra dolça* from the Empordà is made with sugar, lemon zest, cinnamon, and salt and is often served fried with apples.

Two destinations in Barcelona serve well for anyone wishing to sample these riches. The Botifarreria de Santa Maria is one of the city's prime pork butchers, stocking most of the Catalan specialties plus a fascinating range of original *botifarres,* featuring such ingredients as duck liver, fresh garlic, wild mushrooms, and the typically Catalan combination of spinach, pine nuts, and raisins. At La Cansaladeria, near the market in the urban village of Sants, master butcher Jordi Alsina presides as perhaps Barcelona's greatest expert on local pork cookery. He puts this knowledge into daily practice at his modest-sized shop, where he makes most of his *embotits* in the back. His *botifarra d'ou,* sausage with egg, is a delicious specialty worth seeking out if you happen to be in Barcelona at carnival time.

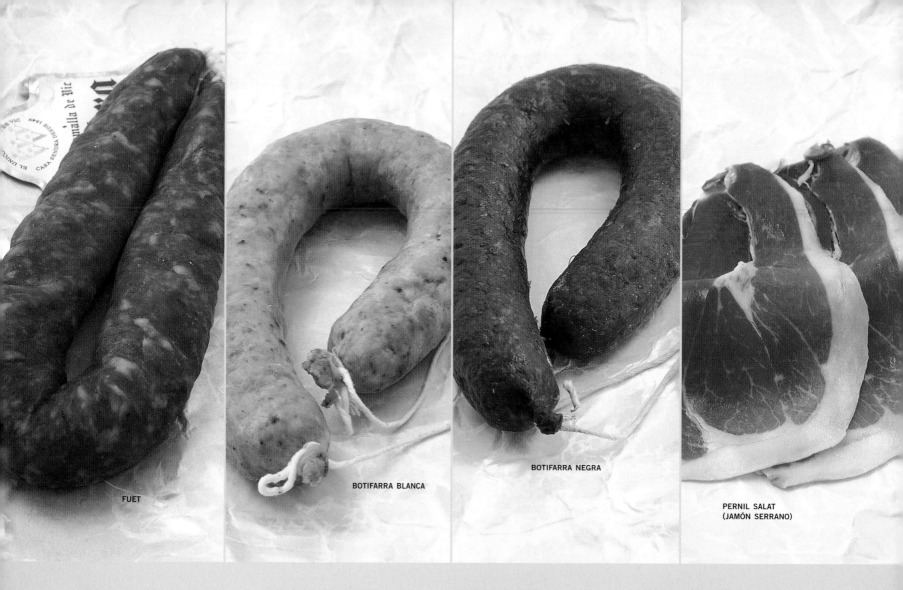

FUET

BOTIFARRA BLANCA

BOTIFARRA NEGRA

PERNIL SALAT
(JAMÓN SERRANO)

FUET

Long, thin, and dry cured, this salami-like sausage is made with white wine, pepper, and spices. It often develops a layer of natural white bloom on the surface. *Fuet* is a favorite for snacking, served, skinned and thinly sliced, with *pa amb tomàquet* (tomato-rubbed bread; page 75) or put into the lunches of schoolchildren. The sausages are almost certain to be found in the picnic basket of any Barcelonan heading out of town for the weekend.

BOTIFARRA BLANCA

This firm, white sausage has been produced for at least four hundred years. Mildly spiced, juicy, and aromatic, it is made with a mixture of lean meat and gelatinous cuts. Some Catalan *xarcuters* like to add egg to the mixture, in which case it becomes a *botifarra d'ou*—a specialty of carnival celebrations, especially in Barcelona. *Botifarra blanca* is usually seared, grilled, or fried and frequently accompanies *mongetes* (stewed white beans).

BOTIFARRA NEGRA

Botifarra negra is the Catalan version of blood sausage, those types made with fatty meat and blood (called *morcilla* throughout the rest of Spain). It often contains minced onion and various spices, including cloves, black pepper, and allspice. Since it has been preboiled, it can be thinly sliced and eaten without further cooking More commonly, however, it is sliced, fried briefly, and served as part of a lunch platter, perhaps alongside eggs and potatoes. *Botifarra negra* is also a vital ingredient in the classic dish *faves a la catalana* (page 113).

PERNIL SALAT
(JAMÓN SERRANO)

This exceptional cured serrano ham, although not in the same league as the best Spanish *pernil ibéric* (page 37), is produced in the Pyrenean town of Olot. Though the qualities of a good serrano ham are not widely known outside of Spain, they are increasingly appreciated. The rich, sweet-salty punch of flavor makes it a natural partner for a dry sherry. Other excellent cured hams can be found outside Catalonia: Jabugo, Dehesa de Extremadura, and Guijuelo are Spain's three great areas of production for *ibéric* ham.

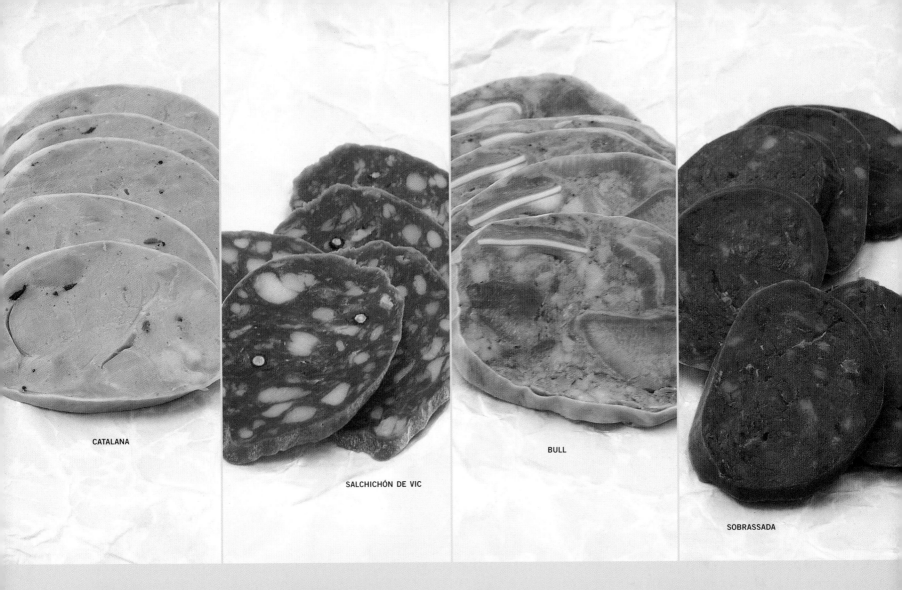

CATALANA

SALCHICHÓN DE VIC

BULL

SOBRASSADA

CATALANA

Many Catalan *embotits* have their equivalents in other parts of Spain. *Botifarra negra,* for example, resembles the blood sausage *morcilla de Burgos. Catalana,* however, is unique to Catalonia. According to some food historians, it may be the oldest of all Catalan sausages. Primarily made of lean meats, it has a firm texture and is generally large in size to make slicing easier. It is often flavored with white wine or black pepper, or in luxurious versions, pieces of black truffle. *Catalana,* like *bull* (see right), makes a superb sandwich filling.

SALCHICHÓN DE VIC

Undoubtedly the best-known Catalan *embotit*—as well as the most prestigious and expensive— this specialty sausage, also called *llonganissa,* is one of the world's great pork products, equaled only by the finest artisan salami from Italy. It is best eaten in thin slices, typically with crusty bread or toast drizzled with olive oil. The recipe, as followed by artisan producers in the town of Vic, is surprisingly simple; the only spices used are salt and pepper.

BULL

The name of this very classic Catalan sausage is derived from the Spanish verb *bullir,* which means "to boil." The raw materials include mainly variety meats from the pig, such as ears, feet, and the parts around the pig's head and jaws. These gelatinous meats help create the dense, sliceable texture of *bull.* The meats are thickly chopped, mixed with spices and pimentón, and stuffed into sausage skins. The sausages are then boiled, cooled, and sliced thinly for eating in sandwiches, on toast, or as part of a mixed Catalan salad (page 122).

SOBRASSADA

Dry-curing meat is impossible in the hot, humid climate of the Mediterranean islands, so the people of Majorca, Ibiza, and Minorca developed another technique: they add large amounts of pimentón to preserve the sausage meat for *sobrassada,* turning it bright orange in the process. *Sobrassada* is found in various forms—thick links in Majorca, thin links in Ibiza, or packed into small tubs. This delicious sausage is perfect with *pa amb tomàquet.*

Olive oil is a cornerstone of all southern European cuisines, and *cuina catalana* is no exception. Celebrated for both its distinctive flavor and healthful properties, it is the basis for almost every savory dish in the Catalan repertoire and is used generously throughout the Mediterranean diet.

OLIVE OIL

Olive oil is an essential ingredient in all the important sauces in Catalan cuisine, namely, *sofregit, romesco,* and *samfaina,* as well as the two eminent emulsion sauces, *maionesa* (mayonnaise) and *allioli* (garlic mayonnaise). Drizzled over toasted bread that has been rubbed with tomato, it is an indispensable ingredient of *pa amb tomàquet* (page 75). It is even beginning to be used by some chefs in Barcelona as an element of the dessert course, in innovations such as chocolate–olive oil cookies and olive oil ice cream.

Olive oil is produced over a wide area of Catalonia, both on an industrial scale and in traditional *almazaras* (small estates). The most common cultivated olive variety is the Arbequina, famed for its exquisite delicacy of flavor. It is relatively small, roundish, and a delicate yellow-green when ripe. Other

varieties grown in Catalonia include Farga, Morrut, Verdiell, Sevillenca, and Empeltre.

Catalonia is not the largest olive oil producer among the Spanish regions; that title goes to Andalusia (which is home to about 60 percent of all the land devoted to olive trees in the country). But for quality, Catalonia's products are hard to surpass. Almost half of all Catalan olive oil is extra-virgin (derived without heat or chemicals from the first pressing) and is made predominantly from Arbequina olives.

Catalan olive oil also has far-reaching historical importance. In 1975, the oil-producing region of Les Garrigues, outside of Lleida, decided to create Europe's first-ever *Denominación de Origen* (DO) for olive oil. The new legislation enshrined in law the special qualities of Les Garrigues oil, such

as its almondy, grassy fragrance. Two types are produced: *afruitat* (fruity), a thick, green oil from the early crop; and *dolç* (sweet), a yellow, more fluid oil. In 1977, the region of Siurana, near Tarragona, followed Les Garrigues in registering as a DO. Oils from Siurana's upland zone are tangy, smoky, and rich, while nearer the coast they are golden yellow and buttery smooth. Both areas continue to be pioneers in the production of single-estate, single-variety, and organic oils. Other important oil-producing DOs in Catalonia are Terra Alta and Baix Ebre.

Every estimable Barcelona food store sells a selection of Spanish olive oils, and local supermarkets such as Mercadona or Caprabo have a good Catalan selection. For the more expensive single-estate designer oils try the Corte Inglés store on Plaça de Catalunya.

Making olive oil is only the final stage in a long process that begins with the planting of the trees. The best orchards in Catalonia are planted deep in well-drained soil. The young trees must be pruned, fertilized, irrigated, and treated for pests. In two or three years, they will begin to bear fruits, and the transformation of bitter, inedible olives into sweet, golden oil begins.

Olive Harvest

The olive harvest takes place in late autumn and winter, at which time the olive-growing areas of Catalonia become a frenzy of activity. Traditionally trees were beaten with long poles so that the fruit fell onto nets spread out on the ground. Nowadays, modernized producers use mechanical shakers with long, vibrating arms in place of the sticks. Neither method is ideal, however, since the olive is a delicate fruit and prone to bruising. For a high-quality oil, the olives must be picked by hand.

Using Olive Oils

When using olive oil in the home kitchen, it's important to match the quality of the oil with the job at hand. In general, a good extra-virgin oil is best appreciated uncooked, in salad dressings; as a condiment for fish, freshly baked bread, or simple steamed vegetables; or drizzled on *pa amb tomàquet*, whereas a less intensely flavored oil is used for frying. (Most Spanish cooks like to fry in abundant olive oil and reserve the oil for future use.) Note, however, the best *maionesa* (mayonnaise) does not call for only extra-virgin oil, as it can make the sauce too green and bitter. Virgin oil (see right) with perhaps a dash of stronger extra-virgin toward the end of the mixing process produces a mild, flavorful *maionesa*.

The issue of freshness is important with olive oil, especially with the finer artisan oils that do not contain any preservatives. Olive oil is a surprisingly delicate product and can oxidize quickly once exposed to air and light. The best oils should be purchased as soon as possible after pressing and stored in a cool, dark place.

Making Olive Oil

PROCESSING AND GRINDING The olives are cleaned of dirt and leaves within a few hours of harvest to preserve the polyphenols and flavor elements of the fruits. They are then ground, with pits intact, in a traditional stone mill or stainless-steel hammer mill.

PRESSING The resulting paste is spread out onto circular mats that are piled on top of one another and then pressed. Traditional presses used a single heavy tree trunk or a primitive hydraulic system made of cast iron. However, the state-of-the-art Sinolea separator, which extracts oil from the paste by means of stainless-steel blades, is gradually replacing Catalonia's traditional presses.

FLAVORS AND CATEGORIES The first oil to run from the presses is defined as extra virgin. Subsequent untreated pressings are called virgin oil. Finally, the paste is treated chemically to extract the remaining oil, and this yield is often blended with oil from other batches to create *aceite de oliva puro,* an oil that is lighter in flavor and color and more fluid than initial pressings.

It would be hard to overestimate the importance of seafood in Catalan cuisine. You could remove the meat dishes and it would still be a worthwhile and varied cuisine; remove the fish dishes, however, and you take away its heart and soul.

SEAFOOD

Fish in Catalonia was traditionally associated with fasting and particularly with Lent, a time of year when meat was barred from the menu. Some fish types, particularly salt cod, still maintain this link with religion. But as Spain's commitment to Catholicism has gradually softened, so has its attitude toward penitence. Nowadays, virtually everyone knows the health benefits of fresh fish, and Catalan fish markets are busier than ever.

La cuina catalana uses fish in a broad range of cooking techniques, from frying and boiling to roasting and grilling *a la brasa* (over coals). Some of Catalonia's most delicious preparations of white fish, such as grouper and gilthead bream, involve baking the whole fish in the oven, either encased in rock salt (page 161) or laid on a bed of thinly sliced vegetables like potatoes and red bell peppers (capsicums), generously sluiced with olive oil.

Seafood mixed with rice is an equally classic combination along the entire Mediterranean coast, and it sometimes takes unusual forms. *Arròs negre* uses squid ink to turn the dish a sumptuous shade of purplish black, whereas *rossejat* calls for browning the rice in the pan before adding the fish and stock.

It seems that all Mediterranean cuisines have at least one mixed fish soup or stew to their name. Catalan cooking has several. Best known of all is the *suquet,* a simple combination of potatoes and rockfish with a *picada* of almonds and garlic, closely followed by the *sarsuela,* a popular dish in Barcelona that includes a variety of shellfish. Then there are the *romesco* of Tarragona with its almond-hazelnut sauce, the *simitomba* of the Costa Brava (monkfish and potatoes with a thick topping of *allioli*), and the *all cremat* of Vilanova, featuring lots of toasted garlic.

Bacallà (salt cod) is an oddity among the fish species found in Barcelona's markets since cod is generally caught in the cold waters of Iceland or the Faroe Islands and salted for export to Spain and Portugal. Catalan cooking has at least a dozen popular recipes for *bacallà,* including Barcelona's famous *bacallà a la llauna* (oven roasted in a special tin), *bunyols de bacallà* (fritters), and, most classically, with *samfaina* sauce (page 141).

An oddity of a different kind is the Catalan tendency to mix seafood and meat in the same dish, resulting in heady delights known as *mar i muntanya* (page 149).

You can find these riches at the many *peixateries* (fishmongers) in the city. The most plentiful seafood destination is the fish section of La Boqueria (page 25), while the venerable Ricart, a fish shop located in the Barceloneta district, is also a superb source.

Catalan fishmongers take great pride in the rich variety of their stock.

CALAMARS

ESCAMARLANS

GAMBES

MUSCLOS

ESCAMARLANS

Escamarlans (*langostinos* in Spanish, and often referred to as Dublin Bay prawns) are frequently confused with their undersea cousins, *gambes* (shrimp/prawns). They are paler in color and have a more delicate flavor and firmer, meatier texture. The Spanish regard *escamarlans* as superior to shrimp and are prepared to pay a much higher price for them at the market—especially during the holidays, when they are traditionally prepared. They are often served cold, with *allioli* on the side.

GAMBES

Juicy and bursting with the flavor of the sea, *gambes,* or shrimp (prawns), are a favorite food of Barcelonans. They are cooked *a la planxa* (on a griddle, page 95) or *a la brasa* (over coals) or are briefly fried in olive oil. Eat them Spanish style: first snap off their heads and suck out the juices, then peel off the shell from the rest of the body. For the best of the best, seek out the shrimp of Palamós and Roses, two small coastal towns north of Barcelona; these *gambes* are famous for being creamy and succulent.

CALAMARS

Calamars a la romana, battered and deep-fried squid rings, is the classic Spanish treatment for this popular seafood. Squid are also commonly cooked *a la planxa,* simmered with potatoes and onions, or, in the Empordá, stuffed with ham, egg, and an almond *picada.* In upscale restaurants, it is usual to see the designation *de pote,* meaning that the squid has been caught by the traditional hook-and-line method as opposed to the invasive commercial techniques that bruise and damage the delicate flesh.

MUSCLOS

Spanish *musclos,* or mussels, come mainly from the cool waters of Galicia, where they are farmed in the estuaries of the Rias Baixas. Once in Catalonia, they typically find their way into some type of rice dish, or sometimes they are prepared *a la planxa* and tossed with parsley and garlic. A popular tapa in Barcelona presents the cold, cooked mussel in its shell, dressed with a vinegary *pipirrana* of diced red and green bell pepper (capsicum) and tomato.

ORADA

ESCÓRPORA

ANXOVA

ORADA

The *orada* (*dorada* in Spanish) is distinguished from similar species of fish by a small patch of golden color just above the eyes; hence, the English name, gilthead bream (*orada* and *dorada* both mean "golden"). Once an expensive and much sought-after fish, it is now more affordable, thanks to the rise of *piscifactorias* (fish farms) along the Mediterranean coast. The *orada* is the classic choice for roasting whole in the oven, most commonly *a la sal* (encased in salt; page 161) or on a bed of potatoes and onions.

ESCÓRPORA

The *escórpora*, or scorpion fish, is a common sight in the fish markets of Barcelona and in other Mediterranean cities (such as Marseilles, where it is used in bouillabaisse). *Scorpaena scrofa* is an unprepossessing creature, red and covered with fierce-looking spines that are poisonous to the touch—even when the fish is dead. A rockfish that lives close to the shoreline, the *escórpora* is highly valued by Catalan cooks for its rich flavor and gelatinous flesh. It is considered a vital ingredient for any good fish stock.

SARDINES

Few smells are more evocative than that of fresh sardines grilling over an open fire. These small, silvery fish are at their best from June to September, when they are especially fat and meaty. The food fiesta *sardinada popular,* in Calella on the coast near Girona, is a grand celebration (usually in mid-May) of grilled sardines served with *pa amb tomàquet* (tomato-rubbed bread; page 75) and washed down with plenty of wine.

ANXOVA

Anchovies marinated in olive oil, parsley, and vinegar, or *boquerones en vinagre*, are regularly seen in Barcelona bars. They are also served deep-fried, either whole or in fillets. But most commonly they are salted and canned in olive oil, then eaten as a snack on toast, in salads like *xató* (page 109), or as a topping for savory *coques* (flatbreads). The most prestigious salted anchovy preparations in Spain, those of L'Escala near Girona, raise this humble fish to the level of a true delicacy.

As is typical in southern European society, wine is an important part of life in Catalonia. No meal is complete without a glass or two, and even children are sometimes given a drop of wine to taste. It is seen as a natural part of a civilized lifestyle.

CATALAN WINE

The grapevine is, together with the olive tree, the most characteristic element of the Spanish landscape. It grows across the length and breadth of the country and produces wines of every imaginable type. Spain has more land devoted to vineyards than any other country in the world, with a staggering 2.9 million acres (1,180,000 ha), although it is considered only the third most important wine producer, after France and Italy.

The vineyards of Catalonia represent a variety in terms of vine types and ages. Fifty years ago, most of the vineyards in this region were planted with traditional Spanish grape varieties, such as Macabeu, Ull de Lebre, Garnatxa, and Parellada. But in recent years, growers have been influenced by New World grapes, and now Merlot, Chardonnay, and Cabernet have been introduced.

Even though historically Catalonia has not been known as a major wine-growing area, Catalan wines were some of the first made on the Iberian peninsula, pressed from the fruit of vines planted by the ancient Greeks in their colony at Empúries. In the 1950s, most Catalan wine was poor stuff indeed, considered peculiar and somewhat primitive. Even up until the 1970s, most of the local wine was sold in bulk. People would take their bottles to the wineshop, or *bodega,* and fill them straight from the barrel. Wine was either drunk at home as an accompaniment to the large midday meal, or swigged from thick glasses in small, gloomy bars where women never ventured.

In those days, even though vast amounts of wine were produced, most of it was of dubious quality. The plains of the Spanish provinces Castille La Mancha and Murcia, near the town of Jumilla, were the source of industrial quantities of basic table wine—certainly not the kind of wine most Spaniards pour at the table nowadays. Without the benefit of temperature control, fermentation took place at a tremendous speed, effectively burning off the delicate fruit aromas and subtle nuances of the grapes. Spanish reds and whites alike were all too often thinly flavored, lacking body, oxidized, and too alcoholic—the classic "hot country" wine of the past, now consigned to history.

The changes began in the 1960s, with the success of Torres, the principal wine family of the Penedès—an esteemed wine-growing region south of Barcelona—whose table wines were modern products with a worldwide appeal. Since then, Catalan wine

Catalan wine has a history stretching back to the ancient Greeks.

has not stopped improving, and some of the sleepiest areas in the past—the prime example being Priorat—now produce some of the best wines in the world.

Catalonia makes every conceivable wine type, from reds, whites, and rosés to sparkling wines (known as *cavas*), fortified wines and muscats, and local specialties like *vi d'agulla* ("needle wine," so named for its high acidity and slight prickle) and the oxidized *vi ranci*.

The region possesses eleven of the sixty-two Spanish *Denominacions de Origen* (DO) for wine. The DO is a system of controls that states that certain wines may only be made in demarcated areas, from particular grape varieties and using specific techniques. The

regarded sparkling wine, made in the town of Sant Sadurní d'Anoia.

Given the importance of wine in Catalan culture, it has taken a surprisingly long while for wine as a subject deserving of expertise, as well as enjoyment, to take root in Barcelona. But the city is quickly making up for lost time. La Vinya del Senyor, in the shadow of the basilica of Santa Maria del Mar, was one of the first wine bars in Barcelona, and remains one of the best. Its extensive wine list, with more than three hundred options, is updated regularly. When in Barcelona check out La Vinya del Senyor's new branch in the Sarrià district, which has fine tapas as well as a standard à la carte menu. With an

Catalonia is a pioneer in the use of old vines to make wines of great concentration and power—a prime example is the Priorat region, where some vines are over sixty years old.

eleven Catalan DOs range from the huge and commercially muscular Penedès, probably the most dynamic of all Catalonia's wine regions, to the small yet perfectly formed Alella, a tiny area of just over twelve hundred acres (500 ha). The DOs in between cover all bases, from the exclusive Priorat, whose revolutionary wines have taken the international wine world by storm, to relatively humble and little-known names like Conca de Barberà and Pla de Bages. Tarragona, a region southeast of Priorat, has been planted in vineyards since the days of the Roman Empire, when the local products were shipped to Rome's well-to-do residents. The Greeks were the first to recognize the rich soil of Empordà–Costa Brava, today a source of well-regarded dessert wines and rosés. Looking to the future of Spanish wine, up-and-coming DOs include the regions of Montsant and Terra Alta. Mention should also be made of *cava*—Spain's highly

extensive wine list from around the world, Cata 1.81 is one of the most fashionable of the new breed of wine bar, with a striking design and an interesting menu of *raciones*, light meals, to accompany them. Barcelona's *xampanyeries* (sparkling wine bars) are an excellent way to sample a variety of local *cavas*. El Xampanyet is perhaps the most well known and well loved of these, having been in operation since the 1930s.

The increasing local interest in both regional and international wines is also reflected in some exceptional wine shops, notably Viniteca, an old-town boutique owned by the genial Quim Vila, whose knowledge of Spanish wine is practically encyclopedic; and Lavinia, possibly Barcelona's largest wine emporium and almost certainly its most complete, especially where Catalan wines are concerned. All eleven DOs are represented, and the range, as well as the design and atmosphere of the shop, is quite impressive.

The process of making wine in Catalonia is essentially the same as it is in the rest of Spain and Europe. It follows the rhythm of the year, beginning in the depths of winter when the vines are pruned and cared for, continuing through the summer when the grapes ripen, and culminating in autumn when, in a burst of activity, the harvest takes place and the grapes are crushed.

The Harvest

The moment of the harvest depends on a variety of factors: climate and altitude, grape varietal, and whether the grapes are red or white. Grapes may also be left on the vine longer than usual to concentrate their natural sugars in the sun, as in the case of some Catalan *moscatels*. Once they are ready, the grapes are cut from the vines in bunches and transported to the winery as quickly as possible, where they begin their transformation.

Catalan Wine Dynasties

The story of Catalan wine is one of history, tradition, and economic influence. Nobody knows this better than the dynasties that have dominated *el vi català* over time—in some cases for hundreds of years. Some of the most important names in Catalan wine are families that have built up powerful businesses around their own vineyards and cellars. The Torres family of the Penedès is known throughout the world as the creators of a great wine empire. Another preeminent name is Raventós, the influential family behind the Codorníu label, whose *cava* is one of the most popular in Spain. The family bottled its first sparkling wines in the 1870s, many of which they sent off to royalty in Madrid. The Ferrer family of Freixenet, another well-known, highly regarded sparkling wine producer, also boasts a company history that goes back to the nineteenth century. Finally, the Gramona family represents another Penedès wine dynasty that has recently shot to fame as a producer of up-to-date wines like Gessami, Chardonnay, Más Escorpí, and the ice wine Vi de Gel.

Making Wine

CRUSH AND EXTRACTING Once harvested, the grapes are destemmed and crushed, and then the juice is extracted in a press, although red grapes are sometimes left whole to ferment. The traditional method of pressing with the feet is now quite rare, although it is occasionally seen in rural settings.

FERMENTING Next, the juice undergoes fermentation, the process by which the sugars in the grape juice are converted into alcohol by the yeasts occurring on the grape skins. This is usually done in large stainless-steel vats and takes around fifteen days, after which the wine is cloudy and is left to settle until it is clear.

RACKING AND BOTTLING After fermentation, wine is then usually "racked," or poured off from the tanks and separated from the sediment that settles at the bottom. This allows the wine to breathe. Racking may occur several times before the wine is ready to bottle. It is then filtered, bottled, and ready for aging or selling.

CAVA

ALELLA

CHARDONNAY

PENEDÈS WHITE

CAVA

Spain's cheerful national fizz never claimed to have the slightest rivalry with proper French Champagne—despite the fact that *cava* is known in Spain as *champán.* The truth is that the two are very different wines, with Champagne a superior product. Still, the quality of *cava* has soared in recent years, and the best dry vintages are delicious. This sparkler is often associated with celebrations, like weddings and birthdays, and is also served around the holidays with *turróns* (almond nougat).

ALELLA

This wine, essentially Barcelona's house white, has been popular with the nobility of Barcelona since the Middle Ages. The typical Alella is a soft and easy-to-drink wine, refreshingly light and fruity, and is the perfect choice with seafood.

CHARDONNAY

While local varieties like Parellada, Macabeo, Verdejo, and Airen are still the most popular whites, New World grape varieties such as Chardonnay and Sauvignon Blanc are gaining ground following the growing influence of the wines from California and Australia.

PENEDÈS WHITE

Thanks to skillful marketing, the white wine of the Penedès represents what a Spanish white wine should be: lively and full-bodied, yet well-balanced and packed with fruit. The archetypal Penedès white is arguably Gran Viña Sol from Torres, made with the Parellada grape variety and firmed up with a dose of Chardonnay. Other Penedès whites blended with the Chardonnay grape have also shot to international fame—especially Milmanda from Torres, widely regarded as one of Spain's finest white wines.

RIOJA

Rioja is Spain's best-known wine, both within the country and abroad. Despite Catalonia's loyalty to its own vintages, a good Rioja commands a great deal of respect in Barcelona. A glass of this oaky, velvety red wine, made from the Tempranillo and Garnacha grape varieties, is the perfect pairing to a plate of ham, cheese, and sausages. The word *reserva* on a bottle of Rioja means it has aged for at least three years, with one year in oak barrels; *gran reserva* means five years of aging and two years in oak.

RIOJA

PENEDÈS RED

PRIORAT RED

VI RANCI

MOSCATEL

PENEDÈS RED

The most popular red wines in Barcelona hail from the Penedès region, producer both of fruity and unassuming reds and superb, exquisitely made reds such as Mas La Plana from Torres, an all-Cabernet wine that famously beat out Château Latour in a 1979 tasting. Red grape varieties grown in the Penedès include Ull de Llebre and Garnacha, although "foreign" varieties like Cabernet Sauvignon and Merlot are now successfully being used in conjunction.

PRIORAT RED

Dark, thick, and strong—that was the way Priorat was always thought of in the past, so much so that the wines were barely drunk in Spain but were instead sent in bulk to France for blending. Once a little-known inland district, ravaged by poverty and depopulation, the Priorat has undergone a radical transformation thanks to a handful of dedicated young winemakers. The potent wines of Priorat are now recognized internationally. Because they are expensive, however, they are generally brought out only on special occasions.

VI RANCI

This slightly oxidized, mildly sweet red wine is a traditional product aged in barrels at a higher temperature than normal to allow for natural oxidation to take place. It was commonly drunk as an *aperitiu* (aperitif) or digestif (in the small villages of Catalonia it doubtless still is), but is now mainly used in cooking. It is a common addition to meat stews, roasts, and pasta sauces. Well-known makers of *vi ranci* are deMuller in Tarragona and Scala Dei in the Priorat.

MOSCATEL

Catalans have a sweet tooth and like nothing better than a glass of sweet wine at the end of a meal with dessert, in the afternoon with cookies and cakes, or even as an aperitif. *Moscatel,* a sweet and raisiny wine, is sometimes served in a *porrón,* a long-spouted glass drinking vessel, and often accompanies the platter of nuts and dried fruit known as *postre del músic* (page 173). Some of the best *moscatels* come from Alicante, in the far south of the Catalan lands.

In the 1990s, a new generation of Catalan artisans set out to learn the ancient techniques of Spanish cheese making, with promising results. Many of these pioneers are self-taught and most are based in small, remote villages deep in the countryside.

FORMATGE

Catalonia is prime dairy country. The Mediterranean zone has richly varied flora of aromatic herbs and flowers, perfect for goats, and the foothills of the Pyrenees are permanently lush with grass, making them an ideal habitat for cows. In fact, the traditionally made cheese of Alt Urgell-Cerdanya, a superb cow's milk cheese from the Pyrenees, was recently awarded *Denominación de Origen* status, making it the first Catalan cheese to gain this much-coveted recognition.

Three important figures in the artisan cheese movement in Catalonia are Jordi Conejero, whose Suau de Clúa is one of the best new Catalan cheeses (look for his stall at the Plaça del Pi market in Barcelona on the first Saturday and Sunday of every month); Francesc Buscallà, maker of Baridà,

a fine goat's milk cheese; and Eulàlia Torres in Ossera, near Tarragona, creator of Serrat Gros, one of the best goat's milk cheeses in Spain. Montsec, another notable "alternative" cheese, was invented in 1978 by a group of young people in the formerly abandoned village of Clúa, in the province of Lleida.

There are a number of good cheese shops in Barcelona, and more and more artisan products are being stocked every year. Scottish-born Katherine McLaughlin has a small but exquisite selection of Spanish farmhouse cheeses at her little shop, called Formatgeria la Seu, in the Barri Gòtic, and is always on the lookout for local fresh cheeses. She regularly carries the superb washed-rind Tou de Tillers "Roi," as well as Aitona, Suau de Clúa, and Tabollet. Not far away, in the

Born district, is Tot Formatges, which stocks cheeses from France, Italy, and Germany as well as Spain. Another purveyor of local cheeses is Tutusaus, an upmarket deli in the Sarrià area, where you can sit in a dining area to enjoy the store's fine smoked salmon, *embotits* (sausages), and other delicacies along with wonderful cheeses.

For perhaps the best cheese shop in Catalonia, however, you will have to head outside the city to the Pyrenees. Eugene Celery, owner of Formatgeria Eugene in La Seu d'Urgell, is a master *affineur* (cheese ager and vendor) worthy of the best in France. In addition to a fine range of cheeses from across the French border, he stocks most of the new-wave Spanish Pyrenean cheeses, including Baridà, Serrat Gros, and Nevat.

Thanks to young, innovative artisans, the future looks bright for Catalan cheese.

MAHÓN SEMI-SEC

MAHÓN SEC

MATÓ DE
MONTSERRAT

TOU DELS TILLERS

MAHÓN SEMI-SEC

Small brown cows grazing between rambling stone walls are a distinctive feature of the landscape of Minorca. The dairy cow was brought to Catalonia by the British in the eighteenth century, so it is not surprising that the island's signature cheese, Mahón, resembles England's famed cow's milk Cheddar. The distinctive square shape comes from the practice of tying the curds in large square cloths to drain. Mahón semi-sec, aged for six months or less, is a young, firm-textured, mild cheese with a pronounced yellow color.

MAHÓN SEC

Mahón is a single type of cheese that changes in flavor and texture depending on the length of time it is aged. Aged in cool cellars for up to a year, Mahón sec becomes dry *(sec)* and hard, and loses some of its buttercup yellow color. The flavor transformation during aging is striking. Starting out mild and creamy, the cheese becomes intensely flavored, salty, and nutty, with a piquant edge. Mahón sec is often grated over vegetables or pasta or used on a cheese platter, paired with Madeira or tawny Port.

TOU DELS TILLERS

The maker of Tou dels Tillers, Enric Canut, is a well-respected expert on Spanish cheeses. Made from raw cow's milk near the mountain town of Sort in the province of Lleida, Tou dels Tillers is a Brie-like product with a chalky white skin, runny interior, and mildly creamy flavor. This lightly salty cheese is excellent accompanied by a young red wine such as those from the Empordà or perhaps a rosé from Cigales. It is also often used in cooking.

MATÓ DE MONTSERRAT

Mató is the Catalan name for a simple, fresh cheese no more than a few days old. It is often made with cow's milk, but sheep's milk versions are also readily available. Hugely popular all over the region, it is eaten with honey as a dessert or for breakfast, or it is used in cooking, for example, in sweet cheese tarts like *flaó* (page 177). The best-known *mató* is made in Montserrat, near Barcelona.

FORMATGE DE CABRA
EN OLI D'OLIVA

CABRA AMB
PEBRE

GARROTXA

SUAU DE CLÚA

FORMATGE DE CABRA
EN OLI D'OLIVA

In order to mature, cheese needs
air, so if you take away the oxygen,
the process is dramatically slowed
down. Catalans have a particular
preference for fresh, young cheeses
over aged, strong-flavored ones,
which sometimes leads them
to ingenious solutions. When a
cheese is just a few days old, and
firm enough to handle but not
completely solid, it can be rolled
into logs, sliced into "buttons,"
and immersed in extra-virgin olive
oil. This way the fresh cheese
keeps for weeks, while taking on
the fruity richness of the olive oil.

CABRA AMB PEBRE

During the process of drying and
curing, cheese naturally forms a
rind. Over the centuries, Europe's
cheese makers discovered that
rubbing the cheese with certain
products, such as pimentón, wood
ash, or ground black pepper, not
only helped the rind to form but
also preserved the cheese from
attack by bacteria that might alter
the taste or infect the cheese with
harmful toxins. Pepper is rubbed
over goat cheese for *cabra amb
pebre,* a popular preparation in
Catalonia. The peppery oils
preserve the cheese and impart
a spiciness to its mild creaminess.

SUAU DE CLÚA

High in the Montsec mountains is
the tiny village of Clúa—population
thirty-two—where a few young
artisans have settled to live and
work. The man behind Clúa cheese
is Jordi Conejero, who first created
it twenty years ago. Suau de Clúa
cheese comes in flatish rounds.
Made from raw goat's milk, it is
sometimes presented with a coating of ash and is cured for sixty
to ninety days. In its two decades
of life, Clúa cheese has gained in
popularity and prestige, becoming
one of the most famous of the new
generation of Catalan cheeses.

GARROTXA

This goat cheese is commonly
known in Catalonia as *formatge
pell florida* (literally, "flowery skin
cheese") because of the gray
bloom that forms spontaneously
on the rind. It was originally made
in flat, circular clay molds and
is still faithfully produced in that
shape. The two-pound (1-kg)
cheeses are allowed to mature
briefly, for about two weeks, to
develop a softly unctuous, buttery
texture. A layer of wood ash is
sometimes added to the rind to
help to stabilize and preserve the
cheese. Garrotxa is notable for its
faint aftertaste of hazelnut (filbert).

In the towns and cities of Catalonia, the *pastisseria* is an institution. Every moment of the day provides an opportunity to visit—from morning croissants and midday slices of *coca* to afternoon *berenars* and elaborate desserts fit for any celebration.

PASTISSERIES

There is more to the *pastisseries*—literally, "cake shops"—of Catalonia than their name alone implies. Of course, cakes and cookies are their main stock in trade, but many of them also have specialties that set them apart from their competition. Some *pastisseries* have branched out into sweet or savory *coques* (flatbreads), which are usually the territory of the *forns* (bread ovens). Others are known for their croissants, chocolate bonbons, *crema catalana* (burnt custard; page 170), or their expertise with sweets from elsewhere, such as panettone or plum cake. Some shops are more like confectioneries, others mainly bakeries. The *pastisseria* is in essence simply a dispensary of good things to eat that are mainstays on the Catalan table but that require too much time or skill (or both) for most people to make at home.

Given the decline of interest in churchgoing in contemporary Spain, it's surprising how much influence Catholicism still has over daily lives. For example, nearly every Catalan pastry and cookie has its moment in the religious year, from the *tortell de Reis* made for the feast of Epiphany and the *coca de Sant Joan* for the Feast of Saint John to the *turróns* and *neules* for Christmas. This calendar is strictly adhered to; it's useless to look for *mona de Pasqua* (chocolate Easter cake; page 174) in November, for example, or *panellets* (nut cookies; page 80) in April.

By and large, Catalan baking, like the food in general, is not characterized by subtlety or great refinement. Its strength resides in the skill with which even simple things can be made delicious. The basis of the repertoire is a rich brioche dough, and

the difference between one specialty and another is mainly in the variety of fillings and toppings. It has been further elevated by the influence of nearby France, and almost all *pastissers* now use butter, instead of the more traditional lard, for making cakes. (Vegetarians take note, however: *Llardons,* or fried bits of pork, are a common feature of the *coca de Sant Joan* and *coca de Sant Jaume.*)

When in Barcelona, it is well worth taking a tour of some of the city's grand *pastisseries.* Five of the best in town are Escribà, Foix, Brunells, Baixas, and Sacha. They are not only sumptuously decorated but also enormously popular, and it's not uncommon to see lines snaking out the front door onto the street. If your purchase is a gift, say so *("es per regalar")* and it will be packed up in a box with ribbons and bows at no extra charge.

Borreguets Sant Antoni
2'00€ bo/su

Panellets
assortits

Sweet and savory treats draw crowds at Barcelona's finest *pastisseries*.

BRUNEL

The *coca* is Catalonia's most famous pastry. It takes many forms, both sweet and savory, from the roasted vegetable–topped *coca de recapte* (page 76) to the sugary *coca de vidre* (page 91). *Les coques* are popular foods all year long but are particularly abundant during the processions and parties held during carnival.

Types of Coques

The word *coca* signals a pastry base. From the popular *coca de recapte,* topped with anything from peppers to salted herrings to sausages, to the typical Balearic Islands' *coca,* topped with spinach, pine nuts, and raisins, what characterizes *coques* is variety. They can be sweet or savory, crowned with cinnamon and lemon, glacéed fruits, nuts, cheese, mushrooms, ham, anchovies, or tuna and tomatoes. Others are filled with such delectables as shredded pumpkin or custard.

Escribà

Tourists walking down the Ramblas market street in the heart of Barcelona often stop in amazement at the jewel-like Pastisseria Escribà. The beautiful gold-and-green art nouveau storefront acts as a magnet for anyone interested in early-twentieth-century design. Once you enter the shop, however, academic concerns take second place to appetite. Escribà is a treasure trove of fine sweets both local and foreign, with a bounty of almond cookies, sugary *coques* studded with pine nuts, and specialties like *brazo de gitano* (gypsy's arm), a cream-and-sponge-cake roulade, or *rambla,* a biscuit-and-chocolate truffle cake. The members of the Escribà family are the aristocrats of Barcelona *pastissers.* The business was founded in 1906, and Antoni Escribà, the patriarch of the firm, is as famous in Catalonia as chef Ferran Adrià. He even has his own entry in the Catalan national encyclopedia: "A man of great culture and sensibility."

Making Coca de Llardons

MAKING THE PASTRY *Coca de llardons* is the quintessential Catalan *coca,* simple and delicious when freshly made with the best materials. The basic ingredients are flour, butter or lard, minced pork fat or *panceta* (the *llardons*), sugar, and pine nuts. First, the dough—flour, butter or lard, salt, and water—is mixed, then kneaded by hand.

ROLLING AND DIVIDING Next, the dough is rolled out into a thin sheet, the *llardons* are sprinkled on top, and the dough is folded over and rolled out again. It is then divided into pieces, and each piece is then rolled out one last time into an elongated strip with rounded ends—the shape of the classic Catalan *coca.*

FINISHING AND BAKING The shaped pastries are finally brushed with melted lard or butter and generously sprinkled with sugar and pine nuts. They are then baked at a high temperature until the sugary topping is browned and crispy, which takes about 20 minutes. The *coca de llardons* is best eaten warm, with a steaming cup of hot chocolate or coffee, or a glass of sparkling *cava. Salut!*

The affair between chocolate and Barcelona has been going on for centuries. The city has had a close and fulfilling relationship with *xocolata* since at least 1759, when Carlos III arrived from Naples in a galleon and handed out gifts of chocolate powder to the crew members as a sign of gratitude.

XOCOLATA

The custom of enjoying chocolate as a beverage is a deep-rooted one, still very much alive in Catalonia. Drinking chocolate is thick and sweet, just right for dunking with *churros* (long fried pastries), *magdalenas* (madeleines), or, most typically in Barcelona, *melindros,* sponge cake topped with icing.

But chocolate in Catalonia has more unpredictable uses. For example, it may appear in a stuffing for squid, and it forms part of the *picada* used in the complex *mar i muntanya* dishes of northern Catalonia (see page 149). Dark chocolate is grated into game stews as well, where it adds a rich smokiness and helps thicken the liquid.

Chocolate in solid form is eaten habitually in Catalonia, though perhaps not in quantities as large as in those cultures farther north. Brunells, a *pastisseria* founded in 1852 and whose original wood-fired oven is still in use, sells a brown paper–wrapped chocolate bar containing 75 percent fine cacao from Venezuela, Ecuador, and Grenada. Other well-known local brands are Solé, Simon Coll, Blanxart, Xoco-Ter, Ludomar, and Cudié. The last is also famous for its bonbons.

Beyond the standards, however, a quiet revolution is taking place in and around Barcelona. The city is discovering, along with the joys of eating and drinking fine chocolate, the arts of the praline, the truffle, and the artisan bar. A chocolate culture is developing, one that puts increasing emphasis on quality and craft. Shops such as Xocoa and Cacao Sampaka (the latter calls itself *El Nou Mercat del Cacao*) offer chocolate lovers an exciting and appetizing mixture of design and gastronomic thrills, with truffles flavored with balsamic vinegar, olive oil, hazelnuts (filberts), and even anchovies. Elda, a town in southern Valencia, boasts one of Europe's magisterial chocolate makers in Paco Torreblanca, winner of many awards for his exquisite workmanship. Chocovic, a shop making *couverture* and fine eating chocolate in the town of Vic, is shaping up as a worthy competitor for French firms such as Valrhona.

Chocolate desserts, the more chic the better, are all the rage in Barcelona. There are few cities in the world where a restaurant that serves only desserts (the most famous being Espai Sucre, run by chef Jordi Butrón) could be a stunning success. Likewise, at the height of fashion, Oriol Balaguer's new "showroom," as he calls his workshop in Barcelona, is a minimalist temple to the exquisite art of chocolate.

Chocolate culture in Barcelona is a mix of traditional and avant-garde.

Chocolate truffles and other soft-centered bonbons have always been popular in Barcelona, and a box of beautiful chocolates is a common gift when having dinner at a friend's home. The city's new wave chocolate shops like Xocoa have taken the traditional bonbon, slimmed it down in size, and transformed it into an elegant, finely made, and expensive delicacy.

Changing chocolate culture

The culture of chocolate in Barcelona has grown dramatically in the last ten years. In the old days, chocolate came in two basic forms: *chocolate a la taza,* a slab of bitter chocolate to be grated and mixed with water or milk for drinking, and the traditional truffle. Modern tastes have changed. Barcelona now prefers its chocolate in the form of a bar, and as bitter as possible: 75 percent, 85 percent, and even 100 percent cacao are possible.

Xocoa

Although it might not look like it from the ultramodern design of each of the shops, Xocoa is one of Barcelona's oldest chocolate firms with a history going back to 1897, when the Escursell family established its first shop in the Barceloneta neighborhood.

Nowadays, the business is run by grandsons Miquel and Marc, who have three shops located around the city and a restaurant specializing in both sweet and savory crepes. The restaurant is notable for both the food and its design, particularly the elegant "white chocolate" chairs. The brothers have branched out daringly from the traditional repertoire of truffles and pastries into novelties like herb- and spice-flavored chocolates, chocolate-and-saffron mousse, and chile-spiced chocolates, and they also sell candles and incense infused with cocoa. Their chocolate CDs (sold in proper CD jewel boxes) have been a notable hit with clients. Marc and Miquel now plan to make *monas de Pasqua* (chocolate Easter cakes, page 174) with famed local chocolate designer Jordi Labanda.

Making Chocolate Bonbons

MIXING THE FILLING For a classic chocolate bonbon, the first task is to mix the filling, usually either an almond-based praline or a rich ganache of cream and cocoa powder with added flavoring. The mixture is spread out on trays to cool, then cut to the required size.

TEMPERING The next step is to make the chocolate coating for the bonbon. *Couverture* ("covering" in French), which is essentially unflavored chocolate high in cocoa butter, is used. It must be tempered by heating it to 104° to 113°F (40° to 44°C) and then cooled by spreading the melted chocolate on a marble slab. Tempering gives the chocolate an attractive shine and consistent color.

DIPPING AND FINISHING The *couverture* is now melted again so that the bite-sized squares of filling can be hand-dipped in the chocolate. Some bonbons are left plain; others are sprinkled with cocoa powder, nuts, gold leaf, or other decorations. Finally, the bonbons are left to cool and set.

BERENARS I TAPAS

From sweet to savory, snacks and small plates like marinated sardines,

empanadas, and pine nut cookies offer convenience for a fast-paced city.

Food in Barcelona is often a movable feast, to be picked up and savored on the go. One prime source of "fast food" is the *pastisseria,* or pastry shop (page 62), for the sweets Catalans favor at all hours of the day and for savory *berenars* (snacks) like *coca de recapte,* flatbread with any number of toppings. The tapas bar, although not traditional in Catalonia, is now a fixture among Barcelonans who appreciate the convenience of this unique style of Spanish eating. *Berenars* may even challenge the supremacy of a regular three-course meal. A simple, delicious repast can be made from *pa amb tomàquet,* a slice of ham, and slabs of cheese and quince paste.

PA AMB TOMÀQUET
Tomato-Rubbed Bread

Bread and tomato—how something so simple and apparently artless could have come to such importance is one of the mysteries of Catalan food. More than just a dish, pa amb tomàquet is a sign of national identity. Although it can be served year-round, it is particularly good in summer, when tomatoes are ripe, sweet, and full of color, and in winter, when fresh olive oil is running off the presses and still has its fruity taste and golden color. Pa amb tomàquet makes a brilliant party food when served with salamis, pâtés, and cheeses.

1 Prepare a fire in a charcoal grill, preheat a gas grill to high, or preheat the broiler (grill).

2 If using *ciabatta,* slice it crosswise into 4–6 pieces, then, cut each piece in half horizontally. Place the bread on the grill rack or on a baking sheet. Grill or broil, turning once, until golden brown on both sides, about 2 minutes on each side.

3 While the toasts are still warm, rub them on one side with the cut sides of the garlic halves, if using. Cut each tomato in half. Rub the cut sides of the tomato halves on top of the toasts until only the skins are left, then discard the skins. Drizzle with olive oil and sprinkle with salt to taste. If using sliced sourdough, cut the toasts in half. Pile up all the toasts on a serving platter or in a shallow bowl and serve.

Serve with a young, flavor-packed, lightly chilled red wine from the Penedès.

1 *ciabatta* or 8 slices coarse country white bread, preferably sourdough, about ½ lb (250 g) total weight

4 cloves garlic, halved (optional)

4 small, ripe tomatoes, about ⅓ lb (5 oz/155 g) total weight

Extra-virgin olive oil for drizzling

Salt

Makes 4 servings

Pa amb Tomàquet

The custom of rubbing bread or toast with tomato and dressing it with olive oil and salt lies close to the heart of the Catalan way of life. *Pa amb tomàquet,* literally "bread with tomato," has clear links with other Mediterranean customs, particularly Italian bruschetta. But the Catalans' passion for this simple food is unrivaled. *Pa amb tomàquet* is often the first thing to be brought to the table. It is a classic accompaniment for barbecued meat and fish. Along with ham, cheeses, and pickles, it is sometimes presented as a meal in itself. In fact, it is quite common for a basket of toasted bread, a bowl of tomatoes, and a bottle of oil to be placed on the table for guests to construct their own.

When the Catalan food magazine *Descobrir Cuina* asked famous Catalan chefs to come up with their own versions of *pa amb tomàquet,* the results revealed their personal style. Carles Gaig placed fresh tomato pulp in a cone of crispy bread; Carme Ruscalleda combined bread and tomato in a single spoonful; and Ferran Adrià created a tomato ice cream with a wafer-thin bubble of pastry.

COCA DE RECAPTE

Flatbread with Eggplant, Peppers, and Olives

Barcelona's pastisseries don't serve only sweet things. Whatever the day or time of year, there will always be a few savory snacks to take away—usually a tasty coca *baked on the premises, with a topping of eggplant and bell peppers, onions and raisins, spinach and pine nuts, cured anchovies, or wild mushrooms and herbs. The* coca *is typically described as a Catalan version of pizza, with its base of thin, baked crust, though the topping rarely includes cheese and only occasionally features tomato. Sweet* coques *are also made for holidays and other celebrations. This recipe is a version of* coca *most often seen in Barcelona's pastry shops.*

1 red bell pepper (capsicum)

1 green bell pepper (capsicum)

1 eggplant (aubergine)

FOR THE DOUGH

1⅔ cups (8½ oz/265 g) all-purpose (plain) flour

½ teaspoon salt

2 teaspoons baking powder

½ tablespoon olive oil

1 egg yolk

¾ cup (6 fl oz/180 ml) water

1 clove garlic, crushed

12 black olives, pitted and coarsely chopped

Salt and freshly ground pepper

2 large, ripe tomatoes, cut into thin slices

4 tablespoons (2 fl oz/60 ml) olive oil

Makes one 12-by-9-inch (30-by-23 cm) *coca*, or 6 servings

1 Preheat the oven to 450°F (230°C). Place the bell peppers and eggplant on a baking sheet and roast, turning several times to cook evenly, until the peppers are blistered and blackened all over and the skin of the eggplant is wrinkled and shriveled, about 45 minutes. Transfer the peppers and eggplant to a paper bag. Close the bag and set aside until cool enough to handle, about 15 minutes. Leave the oven on.

2 When cool enough to handle, peel off the charred skins of the roasted vegetables. Slice each bell pepper in half lengthwise and discard the seeds, ribs, and stems. Cut the peppers and eggplant into thin strips.

3 While the vegetables are cooling, make the *coca* dough. Sift the flour, salt, and baking powder into a bowl. Make a well in the flour and add the olive oil and egg yolk. Gradually add the water, mixing the wet ingredients into the flour little by little with a wooden spoon. Knead the dough on a lightly floured board until soft, smooth, and elastic, about 1 minute. Form the dough into a ball and place in a large, lightly oiled

bowl. Cover with a kitchen towel and leave in a warm place until the dough puffs slightly, about 30 minutes.

4 In another large bowl, combine the eggplant and bell pepper strips with the garlic and olives and season generously with salt and pepper.

5 Lightly oil a 12-by-9-inch (30-by-23 cm) rimmed baking sheet. On a lightly floured work surface, roll out the dough into a rectangle to fit the pan. Press into the prepared pan and trim away any excess dough.

6 Cover the dough base with the tomato slices. Drizzle 2 tablespoons of the olive oil over the tomato slices. Arrange the eggplant mixture evenly over the tomatoes, and drizzle with the remaining oil.

7 Bake the *coca* until the edges are beginning to brown, about 25 minutes. Remove from the oven and let cool slightly. Cut into squares and serve warm.

Serve with a smooth, fruity Rioja.

ENTREPANS AMB FORMATGE FRESC, ANXOVES I PEBROT

Sandwiches with Fresh Cheese, Anchovies, and Roasted Peppers

Snacks and appetizers like tapas have always been a vital element of the Catalan way of life. The bocadillo *is the Spanish sandwich, a giant hunk of bread stuffed with ham,* salchichón, *chorizo, cheese, deep-fried squid rings, or whatever else takes your fancy. In Barcelona, the* bocadillo *is called by the name* entrepà, *literally "between bread," and a host of "fast-food" joints have sprung up to cater to its enormous popularity.* Entrepans *are eaten any time of the day, but especially in late morning, in the late afternoon, and late at night.*

1 Preheat the oven to 450°F (230°C). Place the bell peppers on a baking sheet and roast, turning several times to cook evenly, until the skins are blistered and blackened all over, about 45 minutes. Transfer the peppers to a paper bag. Close the bag and let the peppers steam until cool enough to handle, about 15 minutes. Peel off the charred skins. Slice each bell pepper in half lengthwise and discard the seeds, ribs, and stems. Cut the peppers into strips and set aside. (The roasted peppers will keep for up to a week in the refrigerator with a covering of olive oil.)

2 Preheat the broiler (grill). Slice each length of baguette in half horizontally. Transfer the baguette halves, cut side up, to a baking sheet and lightly toast under the broiler for about 1 minute. Slice each tomato in half. Rub the cut sides of the tomato halves on the toasted baguette surfaces until only the skins are left, then discard the skins. Drizzle with olive oil and sprinkle with salt to taste.

3 Divide the cheese slices evenly among the bottom halves of the baguette lengths, followed by the roasted bell pepper strips and anchovies. Cover each with the top halves of the baguette lengths and press gently to secure the filling. Cut each sandwich in half again, if desired, and serve at once.

Serve with a glass of ice-cold San Miguel beer.

2 large red bell peppers (capsicums)

2 baguettes, cut into 6-inch (15-cm) lengths

4 small ripe tomatoes

Extra-virgin olive oil for drizzling

Sea salt

4 slices fresh goat's or cow's milk cheese such as queso fresco de Burgos, each ¼ inch (6 mm thick)

8 olive oil–packed anchovy fillets

Makes 4 sandwiches

Anchovies

The little port town of L'Escala on the northern Costa Brava is to anchovies what Palamós is to shrimp (page 95). L'Escala is both the capital of the catch and a byword for high quality. The anchovies are fished at night, brought into the harbor in the morning, and then auctioned at the fishmarket to local companies. The main brands are Callol i Serrats, Casa Bordas, Soles, El Xillu, and Magdalena Sureda (the last is filleted and cured in salt). They are then sold ready for use in olive oil or preserved in salt. Salt-packed anchovies are considered to be of superior quality, but they must be rinsed of excess salt and marinated in olive oil before use.

Anxoves de L'Escala are acknowledged throughout Spain as the finest preserved anchovies on the market, and it's not hard to see why. Experiencing these fat juicy, flavorful fish is a revelation. L'Escala anchovies lend themselves to a variety of culinary uses, from *coca* toppings to salads, but the best way to enjoy them is *au naturel,* on a slice of toasted country bread that has been liberally coated with olive oil and topped with a tomato slice.

PANELLETS DE PINYONS
Almond and Pine Nut Cookies

The first day of November is All Saints' Day in Catholic countries, and Barcelona celebrates it with special foods. Roasted chestnuts and baked sweet potatoes are sold at street stalls. Lines form in the pastisseries for one of the city's greatest delicacies, little, round almond cookies that are similar to macaroons. Classic panellets are sweetened ground almonds bound together in a dough. This is the original version, encrusted with pine nuts. Nowadays, the dough may be flavored with myriad ingredients, from whiskey to candied chestnuts, and might be coated with coconut, chocolate, marzipan, or a variety of nuts.

1 small russet potato, about ¼ lb (125 g), peeled

1 lb (500 g) blanched almonds

Grated zest of ½ lemon, finely minced

2 cups (1 lb/500 g) sugar

1 cup (8 fl oz/250 ml) water

Unsalted butter for greasing

1 large egg white

½ cup (2½ oz/75 g) pine nuts

Makes about 20 cookies

1 Bring a small saucepan three-fourths full of water to a boil. Add the potato and cook until tender when pierced with a knife, about 10 minutes. Drain and transfer to a small bowl. Mash with a fork and set aside to cool slightly.

2 In a food processor, finely grind the almonds. Transfer the almond flour to a bowl. Add the mashed potato and lemon zest and mix thoroughly.

3 In a small, heavy-bottomed saucepan, stir together the sugar and water until the sugar is dissolved. Bring to a boil over high heat, stirring with a wooden spoon until the mixture thickens to a syrup, then stop stirring. Continue cooking until the syrup registers 250°F (120°C) on a candy thermometer (the hard-ball stage), then remove from the heat.

4 Pour the syrup in a thin stream onto the almond mixture, mixing well with the wooden spoon. (Be careful at this point, as the dough will be too hot to handle.) Let cool for at least 15 minutes. Form the dough into a ball, place in a covered bowl or wrap in plastic wrap, and refrigerate overnight.

5 Preheat the oven to 475°F (245°C). Butter a baking sheet.

6 In a small bowl, lightly beat the egg white. Using your hands, shape the dough into balls about the size of a small walnut. Roll each ball in the egg white and then in the pine nuts, embedding the nuts slightly into the surface so they don't fall out during baking. As the balls are formed, place them about 2 inches (5 cm) apart on the prepared baking sheet.

7 Bake the cookies until they are golden brown, 15–20 minutes. Let cool on the pan on a wire rack. Store in an airtight container for up to 1 week.

Serve with coffee after lunch or in the afternoon with a cup of tea or a glass of moscatel.

PA DE FETGE

Country-Style Pâté

This pâté originated in the mountainous landscapes of the Cerdanya region but has since gravitated south to Barcelona, where it appears on charcuterie platters in the city's better tapas bars. Traditionally, this pâté is wrapped in pig's caul, the delicate lacelike fat that surrounds the pig's stomach, and baked; hence the name pa de fetge, *which means "liver bread." It's an easy-to-make country pâté, which owes a major debt to the* pâtés de campagne *of neighboring France. Serve it with salad greens, toasted walnuts, pickles, and warm toast.*

1 In a bowl, soak the bread in the milk for 2 minutes. Squeeze out the milk, then mince the bread.

2 In a large bowl, combine the pork liver, pork fillet, and *panceta*. Add the eggs, minced bread, Cognac, parsley, garlic, pimentón, cinnamon, coriander, thyme, 1 heaping teaspoon salt, and a little pepper. Mix everything together thoroughly.

3 Preheat the oven to 425°F (220°C). Line a 1-qt (1-l) terrine with the bacon slices, laying them across the mold and letting the ends hang over the sides, or line the terrine with the caul. Spoon in the pâté mixture, pressing down gently to prevent air bubbles from forming. Fold over the bacon or caul, enclosing the pâté.

4 Place the terrine in a baking pan and add boiling water to reach halfway up the sides of the mold. Bake, uncovered, until the top begins to brown, about 45 minutes. Cover and continue to bake until cooked through, about 45 minutes longer. Let cool completely.

5 To make the pâté compact and easily sliccable, cut a piece of cardboard to fit inside the dish and wrap it with aluminum foil. Place it on the surface of the pâté and place a heavy weight on top. Transfer to the refrigerator to chill for at least 12 hours or up to 24 hours.

6 To serve, remove the weight and cardboard and turn the pâté out onto a serving platter. If the pâté won't come out of the terrine, warm the base in a bowl of hot water, and try again. Slice and serve.

Serve with an elegant Chardonnay from the Penedès.

2 slices coarse country white bread, about 2 oz (60 g) total weight, crusts removed

½ cup (4 fl oz/125 ml) whole milk

7 oz (220 g) pork liver, trimmed and minced

10 oz (315 g) pork fillet, minced

14 oz (440 g) *panceta* or unsmoked bacon, minced

3 large eggs, beaten

1 tablespoon good-quality Cognac

Generous handful of fresh flat-leaf (Italian) parsley leaves, minced

4 cloves garlic, minced

1 teaspoon pimentón or sweet paprika

1 teaspoon ground cinnamon

1 teaspoon ground coriander

1 teaspoon fresh thyme leaves

Salt and freshly ground pepper

16 thin slices bacon or 1 pig's caul

Makes 8 servings

French Influences

It would be surprising if neighboring France had not had some influence on the Catalan kitchen. The onion soup of the Pyrenees is clearly borrowed from French cuisine, and the *pa de fetge* of the Cerdanya is in essence a classic French *pâté de campagne*. There is even a suggestion that the name of the traditional Catalan salad, *xató,* comes from the French word *château.* Nowadays, however, while French cooking is still highly respected, it has lost some ground to the increasingly exciting new Spanish cooking. During the nineteenth and early twentieth centuries when bourgeois French cuisine was at its apogee, Barcelona was proud to possess an upscale French establishment like Le Grand Restaurant de France. Today, there are still French cooks in Barcelona, such as Jean-Louis Neichel and Jean Luc Figueras, but the tables have turned. "The great Catalan cooks of today have emancipated themselves, and while they are grateful for services rendered, they are now saying farewell to France and proposing new...Mediterranean and Catalan pleasures," writes Barcelona food critic Jaume Fàbrega.

EMPANADA DE PEBROTS I TONYINA

Sweet Pepper and Tuna Pie

Barcelona is a glorious melting pot of cultures. Waves of immigration starting in the mid-twentieth century included regional migrations, such as the Galicians. In the Raval neighborhood, near the Ramblas, many Galician-owned bars are still functioning as they did in the 1950s, serving up traditional menus like octopus salad, boiled pork, sweet almond tarta de Santiago, and bowls of Ribeiro wine. Empanadas are a favorite Galician-inspired snack that can be bought at pastry shops all over the city. These squares of pastry hold various fillings, such as this tuna and bell pepper combination, or spinach, raisins, and pine nuts.

FOR THE DOUGH

3¼ cups (1 lb/500 g) all-purpose (plain) flour

1 large egg

¼ cup (2 fl oz/60 ml) olive oil

4 tablespoons (2 oz/60 g) chilled unsalted butter, cut into ¼-inch (6-mm) pieces

½ teaspoon salt

4 teaspoons baking powder

½ cup (4 fl oz/125 ml) whole milk

FOR THE FILLING

¼ cup (2 fl oz/60 ml) olive oil

1 large yellow onion, finely chopped

2 red bell peppers (capsicums), seeded and finely chopped

6 small, ripe tomatoes, about 1½ lb (750 g) total weight, cored

10 oz (315 g) olive oil–packed, canned tuna, drained

3 hard-boiled eggs

Leaves from 3 or 4 fresh flat-leaf (Italian) parsley sprigs, minced

Salt and freshly ground pepper

Milk for brushing

Makes 8 servings

1 To make the dough, sift the flour into a large bowl. Make a well in the flour and break the egg into it. Beat the egg lightly in the well, then add the olive oil, butter, salt, and baking powder and work them into the flour with your fingertips. Add the milk and mix with your hands until the dough pulls together, adding a little more milk if needed. Knead until the dough is smooth and elastic, about 1 minute. Form into a ball, cover with a clean kitchen towel, and refrigerate for at least 30 minutes or up to 1 hour.

2 Meanwhile, make the filling: In a large frying pan over medium heat, warm the olive oil. Add the onion and bell peppers and sauté until the onion is softened and takes on a deep golden color from the peppers, about 5 minutes. Cut the tomatoes in half and, using the large holes of a grater-shredder, grate the pulp directly into the pan. Discard the skins. Sauté until the tomato darkens in color, about 5 minutes. Using a fork, flake the drained tuna into large chunks, then add to the tomato mixture. Peel and chop the eggs. Add the eggs and parsley to the pan and season to taste with salt and pepper. Cook gently until the mixture is heated through but still moist, about 5 minutes.

3 Preheat the oven to 400°F (200°C). Lightly oil a large baking sheet.

4 Divide the dough into 2 pieces, 1 piece slightly larger than the other. On a lightly floured work surface, roll out the smaller piece with a rolling pin into a 10- to 12-inch (25- to 30-cm) square. Trim and patch the dough if necessary. Place the square of dough on the prepared baking sheet.

5 Spoon the filling onto the dough in an even layer, leaving a 1-inch (2.5-cm) border uncovered around the edge. Using a pastry brush, brush the edges of the dough with milk.

6 Roll out the remaining piece of dough into a square slightly larger than the first square. Carefully lay it on top of the filling and gently press the edges together with your fingers. Roll the edges inward, toward the center of the pie, to seal and form a narrow rim. Brush all over with milk; this will give the crust a shiny, golden surface. (If desired, a decoration of leaves or other shapes can be made with any remaining dough. Press the shapes onto the top crust and brush with milk.)

7 Bake until golden, 30–35 minutes. Serve warm or cold, cut into squares.

Serve with a light, cold Spanish beer such as San Miguel, or a fragrant white Albariño wine from Galicia.

VARIANTES

Spicy Marinated Olives with Pickled Vegetables and Garlic

This bar-top snack is commonly served in Barcelona with a midday aperitif. A memorable version is offered at the Bar Mendizábal in Carrer Hospital, a small kiosk decorated in bright 1970s colors, with a miniature terrace. In Spain, variantes *are normally bought already mixed at market stalls specializing in olives and pickles, but they can easily be made at home. Briefly boiling the garlic cloves takes away some of their strong flavor, while giving them a sweet crunchiness. Any olive variety will do, although Spanish olives would be more authentic.*

1 Bring a small saucepan three-fourths full of water to a boil over high heat. Add the garlic, return to a boil, and cook for 3 minutes. Add the carrot, again return to a boil, and cook for 1 minute longer. Drain, then plunge the garlic and carrot slices into cold water. Drain again and peel the garlic (the skins will now come off easily).

2 Transfer the garlic and carrot slices to a glass bowl. Add the olives, onions, and gherkins and mix well. Add the olive oil, vinegar, ½ teaspoon salt, chile powder, pimentón, and thyme and stir gently to coat all the ingredients evenly. Cover and refrigerate the olive and vegetable mixture until well chilled, at least 2 hours or up to 6 hours, mixing once or twice.

Serve with a strongly flavored aperitif such as vermouth or Campari and soda.

12 cloves garlic, unpeeled

1 carrot, peeled and cut on the diagonal into slices ¼ inch (6 mm) thick

24 mixed brine-cured green and black olives, drained

12 cocktail onions in vinegar, drained

12 baby gherkins in vinegar, drained

2 tablespoons extra-virgin olive oil

1 tablespoon white wine vinegar

Salt

Pinch of hot chile powder

½ teaspoon pimentón or sweet paprika

Generous pinch of fresh thyme leaves

Makes 4 servings

Aperitiu

The prelunch drink is a sacred element of Spanish social life. On any given day, friends meet midday over an ice-cold beer, a small tumbler of vermouth, or a glass of wine. While the *aperitiu* (aperitif) is very much alive as a custom, its nature is changing. In the old days, the classic drink was vermouth from a barrel or on tap. But this is now the province of the elderly, which is a shame, because Barcelona has some fine local examples of *vermut*. Nowadays, the drinks of choice are red wine by the glass for the discerning minority, and beer for the majority. The *canya* is a half-pint (250-ml) glass of beer from the tap; if you ask for *una cerveza,* it will probably come in a bottle. The *cerveseria,* or "beer hall," is a relatively new concept imported from Madrid, offering tapas or *raciones* (larger servings of tapas) along with beer on tap. San Miguel, probably the most famous Spanish brewery, is based in Lleida. Other common brands are Cruzcampo, Estrella Damm, Aguila, and Mahou. An interest in *cerveza dorada,* dark beer, is taking off in Barcelona: flavorful brews are served at classic bars like Xampanyet and Quimet i Quimet.

ESCABETX DE SARDINES
Fried Sardines in Vinaigrette

Escabetx, or pickling in vinegar and spices, is one of the oldest means of preserving food. Partridges and pigeons en escabetx were common sights on the banquet tables of medieval Catalonia. Ruperto de Nola's sixteenth-century cookbook, Llibre del Coch, gives recipes for escabetxos of rabbit, eggplant (aubergine), and sturgeon. The technique has persisted in contemporary Spanish cuisine, and these days cold escabetxos appear from time to time on the menu at Barcelona's upscale tapas bars. Although originally used for meat and game, the preparation works well with any oily, strong-flavored fish.

2 lb (1 kg) fresh sardines, filleted

2 cups (10 oz/315 g) all-purpose (plain) flour

Salt and freshly ground pepper

Equal parts olive and sunflower oil for frying

6 tablespoons (3 fl oz/90 ml) olive oil

2 bay leaves

12 peppercorns

3 cloves garlic, crushed

1 teaspoon pimentón or sweet paprika

1 cup (8 fl oz/250 ml) white wine vinegar

Makes 6 servings

1 If your fishmonger has not done so, first prepare the sardines: Hold a sardine by the tail, letting it hang down into a sink full of water, and scrape the scales from the fish by rubbing them off with your fingertips or using the blunt edge of a knife blade, starting at the tail end and working down to the head (the scales will fly in all directions). Rinse well. Clean each fish by snapping off the head and cutting into the cavity on the belly side, from the anal vent up to the head. Run your thumb along the belly to open, then remove and discard the entrails. Using your fingers, loosen the backbone near the tail end and pull it out along with as many of its fine lateral bones as possible, working toward the head, so the fish forms a single flat fillet. Rinse thoroughly and let drain.

2 Place the flour on a plate or in a shallow bowl, season with salt and pepper, and stir to combine. Toss the sardines in the seasoned flour to coat lightly, shaking off any excess.

3 Pour the olive and sunflower oils to a depth of 1 inch (2.5 cm) into a large, heavy-bottomed frying pan and heat over high heat until smoking hot. In batches, add the sardines and fry them, turning once, until golden brown, about 2 minutes on each side. As the sardines finish cooking, transfer them to a *cassola* or heatproof ceramic dish. When all the sardines are cooked, sprinkle with salt and set aside.

4 Clean the frying pan and add the 6 tablespoons olive oil. Warm the oil over medium heat until hot. Add the bay leaves, peppercorns, and garlic and sauté until the garlic is lightly browned, about 3 minutes. Remove from the heat, add the pimentón, and stir once or twice to combine. Add the vinegar and 1 cup (8 fl oz/ 250 ml) water, return to medium heat, and simmer until reduced by one-fourth, about 5 minutes.

5 Pour the contents of the frying pan over the sardines and shake the *cassola* a little to ensure that the vinegar mixture is evenly distributed. Set aside and let cool. The sardines can be served at once, but will be better after a day or two in the refrigerator, where they will keep, tightly covered, for up to 5 days. Bring to room temperature before serving.

Serve with a chilled, very dry *fino* sherry.

AIRE
ACONDICIONADO

COCA DE VIDRE
Sweet Pastry with Pine Nuts

Coca de vidre is a thin sheet of pastry flavored with anise and pine nuts and caramelized with sugar until it is hard and crunchy; hence the name, which translates as "glass coca." You can buy coca at stalls such as the one outside the cinema at Maremagnum, the giant mall down by the old harbor where all of Barcelona seems to convene on Sunday afternoons to take in a movie. The long, thin board of crisp pastry crumbles into shards as you bite into it, showering the pavement with sugary crumbs.

1 To make the dough, sift the flour into a large bowl. Add the baking powder and whisk to combine. Add the milk, salt, sugar, olive oil, and 1 teaspoon anise liqueur. Mix with your hands into a smooth elastic dough. Form into a ball, cover with a clean kitchen towel, and let rest for 20 minutes.

2 Preheat the oven to 425°F (220°C). Grease 2 large baking sheets.

3 Cut the dough into 4 equal pieces. Pull each piece into a thick sausage shape. On a lightly floured surface, roll out each piece of dough until it is as thin as possible (about ⅛ inch/3 mm thick), yet still easy to handle. It should be roughly three times as long as it is wide and have rounded ends. Carefully transfer to a prepared baking sheet. Repeat with the remaining dough pieces.

4 Prick the surface of each pastry all over with a fork and brush the pastries with the 2 tablespoons olive oil. Sprinkle evenly with the pine nuts and the sugar. Bake until golden brown, about 15 minutes. As soon as the pastries emerge from the oven, drizzle them evenly with the ½ cup anise liqueur. Serve warm or at room temperature.

Serve with a glass of semisweet sparkling *cava.*

FOR THE DOUGH

3¼ cups (1 lb/500 g) all-purpose (plain) flour

1 teaspoon baking powder

1½ cups (12 fl oz/375 ml) whole milk

1 teaspoon salt

1 tablespoon sugar

2 tablespoons extra-virgin olive oil

1 teaspoon anise liqueur such as *anis seco,* Pernod, or pastis

2 tablespoons extra-virgin olive oil

¾ cup (4 oz/125 g) pine nuts

½ cup (4 oz/125 g) sugar

½ cup (4 fl oz/125 ml) anise liqueur such as *anis seco,* Pernod, or pastis

Makes 4 pastries, or 8 servings

Sweet Snacks

An entire category of sweet Catalan foods exists that are not desserts, but snacks, "per picar," as they say in Barcelona. Some are closely associated with a place or time of year: *coca de Sant Joan, mona de Pasqua* (page 174), and *tortell de Reis,* for example, are made exclusively for certain holidays and religious observances. *Turrón* (nougat) is eaten at Christmas, and *panellets* (pine nut cookies; page 80), *orelletes* (deep-fried pastry "ears"), and *bunyols* (anise-flavored doughnuts) are much loved fiesta foods.

Even if they have no direct festive link, there is something about these sweets that makes them special and celebratory. *Carquinyolis* (almond cookies) are often dunked in *moscatel* for a luxurious snack. *Dulce de membrillo* (quince paste) is a Spanish favorite often served with cheese but equally delicious on its own. *Pastissets de Tortosa,* little pies stuffed with shredded pumpkin, make a nice breakfast with a big cup of *café con leche.* And a range of sweet *coques,* including *coques de llardons* (sweet pastry with crispy morsels of pork fat; page 65) are favorite afternoon snacks.

CROQUETES DE POLLASTRE I PERNIL

Chicken and Ham Croquettes

There is no point in pretending there is anything authentically Catalan about this dish. Croquetas (croquetes in Catalan) belong in the repertoire of every Spanish housewife, whether in Barcelona or Burgos. The dish has its roots in the economical cooking of a less prosperous time in Europe, when meat was a luxury and to throw away leftovers was unthinkable. In Catalonia as elsewhere, the remains of the Sunday lunch would find their way into croquetes on Monday. Nowadays, these fried morsels are on the menu of nearly every tapas bar in Barcelona. They make a tasty snack at midday or a comforting addition to supper.

3 tablespoons olive oil, plus
more for frying

3 tablespoons all-purpose
(plain) flour

1½ cups (12 fl oz/375 ml)
whole milk

1½ cups (12 fl oz/375 ml)
chicken stock

⅓ cup (2 oz/60 g) finely chopped
cooked chicken meat

⅓ cup (2 oz/60 g) serrano or other
salt-cured ham, finely chopped

Pinch of freshly grated nutmeg

Salt and freshly ground pepper

1 cup (4 oz/125 g) finely ground
dried bread crumbs

2 large eggs, beaten

Makes about 20 croquettes,
or 5 servings

1 In a small, heavy-bottomed saucepan over low heat, combine the 3 tablespoons olive oil and the flour. Cook, stirring constantly, until the flour has absorbed all the oil, 2–3 minutes. Add the milk and stock, little by little, stirring constantly with a wooden spoon. Use a whisk to smooth out the sauce if lumps start to form. Cook the sauce, continuing to stir constantly, until smooth and thick, 10–15 minutes. Remove from the heat, stir in the chicken, ham, and nutmeg, and season to taste with salt and pepper.

2 Pour the mixture into a metal baking pan and let cool to room temperature. Cover with plastic wrap and refrigerate the mixture overnight. By the next day, the mixture will have congealed into a thick paste.

3 Put the bread crumbs in a shallow bowl, and lightly beat the eggs in a second shallow bowl. Using a spoon and your hands, form the chilled paste into short logs 2 inches (5 cm) long and about 1 inch (2.5 cm) in diameter. Roll them once in the bread crumbs, then in the beaten eggs, and then again in the bread crumbs, making sure each croquette is thoroughly coated.

4 Pour olive oil to a depth of 1 inch (2.5 cm) into a large frying pan and heat over medium-high heat until very hot. Slip in the croquettes a few at a time and fry, turning once, until golden brown, about 3 minutes. Transfer to a plate lined with paper towels to drain. Serve at once.

Serve with a robust and plummy Cabernet Sauvignon from Madrid.

GAMBES A LA PLANXA
Griddled Shrimp with Garlic and Parsley

Griddled shrimp are a fixture on the menu, along with paella and grilled fish, at nearly every beach restaurant up and down the Mediterranean coast from the Costa Brava to Alicante. La planxa (plancha in Spanish), a kind of griddle, is arguably the Spanish cook's favorite cooking tool. At its most basic, it is a metal surface that can be heated from below, preferably over an open fire. It has an important advantage over a conventional grill: the juices from whatever is being cooked are retained and concentrated and never drip into the fire.

1 Season the shrimp with salt and pepper and drizzle generously with olive oil.

2 Place a griddle or a large frying pan over high heat until hot. The griddle is ready when a drop of water flicked on the surface sizzles and evaporates instantly. Place the shrimp on the hot surface and cook, turning once, until they are opaque throughout and the shells begin to brown, about 5 minutes on each side. Sprinkle the garlic and parsley over the shrimp; cook, without stirring, for about 30 seconds; and then turn the shrimp one last time. Transfer to a warmed platter and serve at once.

Serve with a crisp, acidic white wine with a slight sparkle, such as Vi d'Agulla from the Empordà.

24 large, fresh shrimp (prawns) in the shell, about 1½ lb (750 g) total weight

Salt and freshly ground pepper

Olive oil for drizzling

4 cloves garlic, minced

Handful of fresh flat-leaf (Italian) parsley leaves, minced

Makes 4 servings

Shrimp

Shrimp are fished at several points along the Spanish coast, but the best shrimp of all, according to the Catalans, are caught by the fishermen of Palamós, a seaport on the Costa Brava. The famous *gambes de Palamós* spend their lives in undersea ditches 800 to 2,600 feet (250 to 800 m) deep. They are caught with dredging nets, brought into the harbor, and washed clean, after which their characteristic intense red color begins to show. (They are known locally as "the red miracle.") Seared briefly *a la planxa* with sea salt and olive oil, these shrimp have a creamy, almost buttery texture and a wonderfully rich, concentrated taste. The fame of the *gamba* has spread far and wide, while, sadly, the creature itself has become progressively more scarce. Once it was common for a fisherman to bring in over two hundred pounds (100 kg) a day; today the catch has fallen to an average of forty pounds (20 kg) or less. Demand therefore outstrips supply, and prices have soared, making the Palamós shrimp one of Catalonia's most expensive seafood items.

ENTRANTS

From oven-roasted autumn mushrooms and hearty spring vegetable and

garlic soup to fresh summer salads, *entrants* are driven by the seasons.

The typical concept of a first course is a dish that is light, usually a soup or salad. But in Catalan cooking and in Spanish food in general, first courses, although served in small portions, are often rich and potent. Because many favorite *entrants* share the heft and appeal of a main course, dishes like meat-stuffed cabbage leaves or fava (broad) beans with spareribs and sausage *(faves a la catalana)* may be offered as either a first course or as a second course with a salad. By the same token, it is not unusual to forgo the second course and make a meal of *entrants*—for example, on a hot day, when cold gazpacho and country bread are ideal.

GASPATXO ANDALÚS

Gazpacho

Barcelona may be the capital of Catalonia, but it is also a dynamic culinary melting pot in which other Spanish regions are well represented. In April, the Andalusian community of Barcelona, the city's largest minority group at one million strong, holds its own version of Seville's famous spring fair. All the ingredients are accounted for—frilly dresses, folk dancing, and fino sherry in vast quantities. As you feast on typical southern foods like pescaíto frito (fried fish) and gazpacho, you have to pinch yourself to remember you're not in Andalusia.

1 Place 9 slices of the bread in a food processor and spoon the vinegar over. Then add the tomatoes, onion, the cucumber and bell pepper chunks, ⅔ cup (5 fl oz/160 ml) of the olive oil, and 1 cup (8 fl oz/250 ml) water and pulse until smooth. Add more water if desired—some people like their gazpacho thick, while others prefer a runnier consistency—and pulse again. Season to taste with salt and more vinegar, if desired.

2 Cover and refrigerate until well chilled, at least 2 hours or up to 4 hours.

3 Meanwhile, cut the remaining 2 bread slices into ½-inch (12-mm) cubes. In a frying pan over medium-high heat, warm the remaining ⅓ cup (3 fl oz/90 ml) olive oil. Add the bread cubes and fry, stirring often, until golden brown on all sides, about 3 minutes. Transfer to paper towels to drain.

4 Just before serving, transfer the gazpacho to a serving bowl and add the ice cubes. Place the diced cucumber, diced bell pepper, hard-boiled eggs, ham, and prepared bread cubes in individual small bowls to serve as garnishes. Pass the bowls at the table for guests to top their soup as desired.

Serve with a crisp, light white wine from southern Spain.

11 slices day-old coarse country white bread, about 10 oz (315 g) total weight, crusts removed

2 tablespoons sherry vinegar, or to taste

3 lb (1.5 kg) ripe tomatoes, peeled and seeded (page 187)

½ yellow onion, cut into chunks

1 cucumber, peeled, halved, seeded, and cut into chunks

1 red bell pepper (capsicum), seeded and cut into chunks

1 cup (8 fl oz/250 ml) extra-virgin olive oil

Sea salt

Handful of ice cubes

FOR THE GARNISH

1 small cucumber, peeled, halved, seeded, and diced

1 red bell pepper (capsicum), seeded and diced

2 hard-boiled eggs, peeled and chopped

2 slices serrano ham, finely chopped

Makes 6–8 servings

Spanish Regional Influences

In a globalized world, it is increasingly difficult to draw fixed boundaries around national cuisines. More and more, the influences from outside determine the development of a particular cuisine. Catalan cooking, like Catalonia itself, has always been open to the cultural currents of a wider world, and now more so than ever. The influences are coming not just from Asia, South America, and Africa, however, but from the rest of Spain as well. Although tapas, the famed little dishes made for snacking with drinks, originated in the south of Spain, they were never part of Catalan life. Yet they are steadily becoming more popular in Barcelona, which now boasts a number of Madrid-style tapas bars. The Basque *pintxo*, a kind of canapé served on trays at Basque bars, is gaining wider acceptance, too. Andalusian and Galician dishes like gazpacho, *pulpo a la gallega* (marinated octopus), and empanadas are also regular fixtures on local menus. All these influences contribute to the rich and varied mixture that makes up Barcelona's food scene.

ALBERGINIES FARCIDES
Stuffed Eggplant

Glossy purple-black eggplants at peak season in Barcelona are so fresh they give off a sweet, sun-ripened aroma. Catalan cuisine has a number of uses for them. They can be stewed with bell peppers (capsicums) and tomatoes for samfaina *(page 141) or grilled for* escalivada *(page 118). In Majorca, they are made into fritters and served drizzled with honey. Perhaps best of all, they can be stuffed and baked in the oven. This recipe originally comes from the Balearic Islands, but it is now a favorite in Barcelona where it makes regular appearances on menus—especially during eggplant season.*

3 small eggplants (aubergines), about 6 oz (185 g) each

Salt and freshly ground pepper

1 tablespoon plus ¼ cup (2 fl oz/60 ml) olive oil

1 yellow onion, finely chopped

6 cloves garlic, minced

½ lb (250 g) ground (minced) pork

½ lb (250 g) ground (minced) veal

4 large, ripe tomatoes, about 1 lb (500 g) total weight, peeled, seeded (page 187), and minced

2 fresh marjoram or oregano sprigs

1 bay leaf

½ cup (4 fl oz/125 ml) half-and-half (half cream)

3 oz (90 g) Mahón, Parmesan, or other hard cow's milk cheese, grated

Handful of fresh flat-leaf (Italian) parsley leaves, minced

Makes 6 servings

1 Cut the eggplants in half lengthwise. Using a spoon, scoop out the flesh into a colander, leaving a shell about ½ inch (12 mm) thick. Sprinkle the shells and flesh with salt. Place the shells cut side down in a separate colander or on paper towels. Let the eggplant drain for about 1 hour. (Salting eggplant draws out its bitter juices.) Rinse in cold water and dry thoroughly.

2 Preheat the oven to 350°F (180°C). Select a shallow ovenproof dish in which the eggplant shells will fit, cut side up, snugly side by side. (This will help them to retain their shape while cooking.) Rub them all over with the 1 tablespoon olive oil. Arrange in the dish and bake until soft, 15–20 minutes.

3 Meanwhile, finely chop the eggplant flesh. In a heavy-bottomed frying pan over medium heat, warm the ¼ cup olive oil. Add the onion and sauté until softened, about 6 minutes. Then add the garlic, chopped eggplant, pork, and veal. Cook, stirring often, until the meat is nicely browned, about 10 minutes. Add the tomatoes, marjoram, and bay leaf and season to taste with salt and pepper. Continue to cook, stirring until the liquid has almost entirely evaporated, about 10 minutes longer. Discard the bay leaf.

4 Spoon the filling into the eggplant shells. Drizzle a little half-and-half over each one and top with the cheese and parsley. If desired, sprinkle with pepper. Bake until the cheese is bubbling and golden brown, 25–30 minutes. Let cool slightly before serving.

Serve with a full-bodied, well-balanced red wine from the Ribera del Duero.

TREMPÓ

Majorcan Summer Salad

Historians tell us that trempó *comes from the medieval Catalan* trempar, *meaning "to dress" with salt, oil, and vinegar—a word that has died out in Catalonia proper but persists on the island of Majorca. This simple summer salad is not really worth making out of season, as the ingredients must be fully ripe and flavorful—and organic if possible. This is only a basic recipe; lettuce, cucumber, olives, and even pears and apples can be added as you like. Serve with a vinaigrette or with a bowl of* allioli *on the side.*

1 To make the vinaigrette, in a bowl, whisk together the vinegar and ½ teaspoon salt. Slowly add the olive oil while whisking constantly. Taste and adjust the seasoning with salt and pepper.

2 Alternatively, make the *allioli:* Using a mortar and pestle, crush together the garlic and ½ teapoon coarse salt until a thick, smooth paste forms. Transfer the garlic paste to a bowl. Using a whisk and beating vigorously and continuously, add the oil drop by drop, then in a thin stream, until the sauce thickens into a golden mayonnaise, about 15 minutes. Add the lemon juice and stir to combine. To make the *allioli* in a food processor, combine the garlic and ½ teapoon coarse salt and process to a paste. With the machine running, slowly drizzle in the oil in a thin stream, until the sauce thickens. Stir in the lemon juice.

3 Place the tomatoes, green onion, and bell peppers in a large bowl and toss to combine. Dress the salad with the vinaigrette, toss well, and serve. Alternatively, serve the salad with a bowl of the *allioli.*

Serve with a spicy, rustic red wine from Majorca.

FOR THE VINAIGRETTE

2 tablespoons red or white wine vinegar

Salt and freshly ground pepper

⅓ cup (3 fl oz/80 ml) extra-virgin olive oil

FOR THE ALLIOLI

12 cloves garlic, peeled

Coarse salt

1 cup (8 fl oz/250 ml) extra-virgin olive oil

1 teaspoon fresh lemon juice

3 large, ripe tomatoes, coarsely chopped

1 thick green (spring) onion, including pale green parts, or 1 small yellow onion, thinly sliced

1 green bell pepper (capsicum), seeded and cut into narrow strips or rings

1 red bell pepper (capsicum), seeded and cut into narrow strips or rings

Makes 4 servings

The Balearic Islands

The islands of Majorca, Minorca, Ibiza, and Formentera (in decreasing order of size) are not part of Catalonia proper but are considered *països catalans* (the Catalan lands), and their culinary traditions and cultures share common roots. A combination of history and circumstance has shaped the cuisine of these islands, allowing them to preserve some of the medieval dishes that have died out in Catalonia itself, such as the *flaó* of Ibiza (page 177) and the *escaldums* (a rich chicken stew) and *menjar blanc* (almond-milk pudding) of Majorca. Minorca has a number of culinary preparations that hark back to its British domination in the eighteenth century, such as *grevi* (gravy) and *piquel* (pickle). According to a widely accepted theory, *maionesa* (mayonnaise) was taken back to France after the brief French occupation of the island. Many local specialties reflect the emphasis on robust foods from these islands, such as *arròs de matances,* a soupy rice and pork dish seasoned with saffron and garlic from Ibiza, or the Christmastime favorite, *salsa de Nadal,* a potent mixture of almonds, chicken stock, chicken and pork fat, sugar, saffron, and spices.

SOPA D'ALL I VEGETALS DE PRIMAVERA
Garlic and Spring Vegetable Soup

Garlic soup is one of the staple dishes of Catalan, and Spanish, rural society. Workers in the fields found it easy to prepare and restorative after a hard morning's harvest. The writer of a 1845 guidebook to Spain commented, "The Catalonians have a national soup, which is made of bread and garlic. . . . The better classes turn up their noses at these odoriferous delicacies of the peasantry." As a dish, sopa d'all is quite simple. But master chef Carme Ruscalleda, of the world-renowned Sant Pau restaurant near Barcelona, has taken this garlic broth a step further, adding spring vegetables for an extra dimension of color and crunch.

Salt

1 cup (5 oz/155 g) shelled fava (broad) beans

½ cup (4 fl oz/120 ml) extra-virgin olive oil

1 head garlic, cloves separated and peeled

8 slices coarse country whole-wheat (wholemeal) bread, about ½ lb (250 g) total weight, crusts removed

Generous dash of red or white wine vinegar

4 large eggs

4 large green asparagus spears, trimmed and chopped into 1-inch (2.5-cm) lengths

4 large white asparagus spears, trimmed and cut into 1-inch (2.5-cm) lengths

1 small head red endive or chicory (curly endive), cored and cut into 1-inch (2.5-cm) dice

1 cup (5 oz/155 g) shelled English peas

Makes 4 servings

1 Unless you are using very small, young fava beans, you will need to remove their tough skins. Bring a small saucepan three-fourths full of water to a boil. Salt the water and add the fava beans. Blanch for 1–2 minutes, then drain and rinse under cold running water. Pinch each bean opposite the end where it was attached to the pod and squeeze; the bean should pop free. Set the skinned beans aside.

2 In a heavy-bottomed saucepan over medium heat, warm ¼ cup (2 fl oz/60 ml) of the olive oil. Add the garlic and sauté until soft, about 3 minutes. Add the bread and fry until evenly browned, about 2 minutes longer. Add 4 cups (32 fl oz/1 l) water and stir briefly to combine. Transfer to a blender or food processor and process until smooth. Season to taste with salt. Return to the saucepan, cover, and keep warm over low heat.

3 Bring a large, deep sauté pan three-fourths full of water to a boil over high heat. Add the vinegar and 1 teaspoon salt. Turn off the heat. Break an egg into a saucer and gently slide the egg into the water. Repeat with a second egg. Alternatively, cook the eggs in an egg poacher. Cover the pan and let stand until the whites are firm but the yolks are still runny, about 3 minutes. Using a slotted spoon, transfer the eggs to a bowl of ice water. Repeat with the remaining 2 eggs. Leave the eggs in the ice water until ready to use.

4 In a wide frying pan over medium heat, warm the remaining ¼ cup olive oil. Add the asparagus, endive or chicory, fava beans, and peas and sauté until just tender, about 6 minutes. Using a slotted spoon, transfer the vegetables to shallow soup bowls, dividing them evenly. Add a poached egg to each bowl.

5 Reheat the bread and garlic broth gently to serving temperature, if necessary. Divide evenly among the bowls and serve at once.

Serve with a velvety, oaked red wine from Valdepeñas.

XATÓ

Escarole Salad with Salt Cod, Anchovies, and Olives

The basis of this salad is a bed of crisp curly escarole, crunchy and satisfying, combined with strips of salt cod, anchovies, tuna, and a scattering of black olives. But the true glory of xató is its sauce, a kind of romesco made with pounded almonds and hazelnuts, nyora peppers, garlic, and olive oil. The genius of the dish is the way the rich, nutty sauce combines with the salty chunks of fish and the satisfying crunch of escarole. A loaf of crusty bread is essential to mop up the delicious sauce left at the bottom of your plate.

1 To prepare the salt cod, place it in a bowl of cold water to cover, cover the bowl, and refrigerate for 3 days, changing the water once a day.

2 To make the sauce, in a dry, heavy frying pan over medium heat, toast the almonds until browned, about 30 seconds. Transfer to a plate to cool. If using *nyora* peppers, let them soak in boiling water for 10 minutes, then scrape the flesh off the skins. Sprinkle the coarse country bread with the vinegar. Using a large mortar and pestle, grind together the almonds, hazelnuts, garlic, the peppers, and the vinegar-soaked bread until a thick, reddish paste forms. Alternatively, process the ingredients together in a food processor, making sure the mixture remains coarse. Add the olive oil in a thin stream, stirring constantly with a wooden spoon, until the ingredients are thoroughly combined and the sauce is just liquid enough to be poured. Season with salt. (The sauce will keep in the refrigerator for 1 week. Use leftover sauce with roast meats or vegetables.)

3 Remove any bones and skin from the salt cod, then shred the meat with your fingers into thin strips. Cut or tear the anchovy fillets into strips. Place the salt cod, anchovies, and tuna in a bowl with the tomatoes and olives and toss to combine. Pour over enough of the sauce to coat everything thickly and toss again.

4 Just before serving, in a large salad bowl, toss the escarole with the salt cod mixture. Serve at once.

Serve with a fragrant, young white wine such as a Spanish Sauvignon Blanc.

6 oz (185 g) salt cod

FOR THE SAUCE

½ cup (2 oz/60 g) blanched almonds

4 *nyora* or *romesco* peppers or ancho chiles, or 1 teaspoon pimentón or hot paprika (see page 186)

1 slice coarse country white bread, about 1 oz (30 g), crusts removed

1 tablespoon red wine vinegar

8–10 hazelnuts (filberts)

4 cloves garlic, peeled

⅓ cup (3 fl oz/80 ml) extra-virgin olive oil

Salt

8 anchovy fillets

6 oz (185 g) olive oil–packed canned tuna, drained and separated into 1-inch (2.5-cm) chunks

2 ripe tomatoes, coarsely chopped

¾ cup (4 oz/125 g) black olives, preferably Arbequina

1 head escarole (Batavian endive), cored and separated into leaves

Makes 6 servings

Fiesta Foods: Xató

Catalonia has always been a food-loving land, but the recent explosion of food fiestas is nothing less than a sociological phenomenon. After the *calçotada* (see page 121) came the *pesolada* in the Maresme district, an event devoted to the humble pea and its use in dishes like *pèsols ofegats* (braised peas). Then came the *botifarrada,* a celebration of *botifarras,* or blood sausages, and the *caracolada* and *sardinada,* celebrations of the snail and sardine, respectively. Not to be outdone, the residents of Vilanova i la Geltrú, Sitges, Cunit, and Vendrell, centers of the dish *xató,* decided to put on their own show, and the *xatonada* was born. It has become a major event, especially around carnival, when towns in the coastal area south of Barcelona celebrate the salad with processions and dances. Most *xatonades* include tastings and a competition in which cooks are invited to submit their own versions.

There are now so many food-related fiestas in Catalonia that the regional government has produced a book, *Agenda Gastronòmica de Catalunya,* which tracks them through the year.

SOPA DE RAP I FARIGOLA

Thyme Soup with Monkfish Medallions

Fresh thyme simmered in water with bread, oil, and salt—nothing more—sopa de farigola belongs to an ancient family of soups in Catalonia and Provence made with parsley, sage, mint, and other fresh herbs. To modern palates, the absence of stock might seem to make the soup much too weak. In practice it can be wonderfully soothing food—pure aromatherapy, as the perfumes of the herbs and olive oil gently penetrate the senses. This version of the dish, using a quick fish stock flavored with a sofregit *of vegetables and adding medallions of monkfish, comes from Margaret Nofre of the Sant Carles restaurant in Tortosa.*

1 lb (500 g) monkfish, red snapper, or other firm-fleshed white fish on the bone, skin and dark membrane removed by the fishmonger

¼ cup (2 fl oz/60 ml) extra-virgin olive oil

1 large carrot, peeled and finely chopped

1 large yellow onion, finely chopped

1 large tomato, finely chopped

4 fresh thyme sprigs

Salt and freshly ground pepper

12 slices baguette or 4 slices coarse country white bread, about ¼ lb (125 g) total weight

1–2 cloves garlic, halved

Makes 4 servings

1 Cut away the fish meat from the bones, leaving some meat on the bones to add flavor to the stock. Cut the fish fillet crosswise into medallions 2 inches (5 cm) in diameter and ½ inch (12 mm) thick. Set the bones and medallions aside separately.

2 Next, make a *sofregit:* In a frying pan over medium heat, warm the olive oil. Add the carrot, onion, and tomato and sauté until the onion is softened and translucent, about 10 minutes. Add the monkfish bones and cook, stirring, for 2 minutes. Reduce the heat to low, add 5 cups (40 fl oz/1.25 l) water, and cook, covered, about 15 minutes. Add the thyme and cook for 5 minutes longer.

3 Remove from the heat and strain the stock through a fine-mesh sieve, pressing on the vegetables with a wooden spoon to extract all the liquid. Return the stock to the pan, season to taste with salt and pepper, and add the monkfish medallions. Bring to a simmer over low heat and cook until the fish is opaque throughout, about 5 minutes.

4 Preheat the broiler (grill). Place the bread slices on a baking sheet and broil (grill), turning once, until lightly golden on both sides, about 2 minutes on each side. While the bread is still warm, rub it on one side with the cut sides of the garlic halves.

5 Place 3 slices of toasted baguette or 1 slice of toasted country bread in each soup bowl and divide the medallions among the bowls. Pour the stock over the fish and serve.

Serve with a fruity, full-bodied Penedès white wine, preferably made from Parellada grapes.

FAVES A LA CATALANA

Catalan-Style Fava Beans

When the first baby fava beans come into season in early spring, Barcelona's cooks pounce on them. All over the city, kitchen hands are put to work shelling the little vegetables, most of which will find their way into one of Catalonia's most celebrated dishes, a mixture of tender fava beans; morsels of pork, bacon, and sausage; and refreshing mint. It's a thoroughly traditional dish, but one that seems modern at the same time. When the beans are fresh and tiny, before the skins turn leathery, they are one of the most delectable foods in the world.

1 Unless you are using very small, young fava beans, you will need to remove their tough skins. Bring a small saucepan three-fourths full of water to a boil. Salt the water and add the fava beans. Blanch the beans for 1–2 minutes, then drain and rinse under cold running water. Pinch each bean opposite the end where it was attached to the pod and squeeze; the bean should pop free. Set the skinned beans aside.

2 In a heavy frying pan over medium heat, warm the olive oil. Add the spareribs and *panceta* and fry until golden, about 10 minutes. Using a slotted spoon, transfer to paper towels to drain. Add the *botifarra* slices and fry until crisp on both sides, 4–5 minutes. Using the spoon, transfer to paper towels to drain.

3 Add the green onions to the same pan and sauté until softened, about 4 minutes. Add the garlic and sauté for about 2 minutes longer. Add the fava beans, stir, and pour in the 1 cup wine. Season with salt and pepper, add the herb bundle, and stir to combine. Place the spareribs and *panceta* on top of the beans. Cover, reduce the heat to low, and simmer, shaking the pan occasionally and adding more wine if the mixture dries out, until the beans are tender, 10–15 minutes.

4 Uncover and mix together with a spoon, adding the *botifarra* slices. Let simmer for 1–2 minutes longer.

5 Stir the shredded mint leaves into the beans. Remove and discard the herb bundle, transfer the beans to a serving dish, and serve with the bread.

Serve with a spicy white wine such as Sauvignon Blanc.

Salt and freshly ground pepper

6 cups (2 lb/1 kg) shelled fava (broad) beans, preferably young, tender beans

½ cup (4 fl oz/125 ml) olive oil

10 oz (315 g) pork spareribs, cut into 1-inch (2.5-cm) pieces

6 slices *panceta* or unsmoked bacon, cut into 2-inch (5-cm) lengths

½ lb (250 g) *botifarra negra* or other blood sausage, thickly sliced

2 small green (spring) onions, white and pale green parts, finely chopped

4 cloves garlic, minced

1 cup (8 fl oz/250 ml) dry white wine, or more as needed

6 fresh flat-leaf (Italian) parsley sprigs, 1 bay leaf, and 3 fresh mint sprigs, tied into a bundle with kitchen string

Shredded fresh mint leaves for garnish

Warm crusty bread for serving

Makes 6 servings

Spring Vegetables

Spring in Barcelona brings a host of pleasures: a stroll down the Ramblas among flower stalls stacked with blooms and birds twittering in their cages; the joyous rituals of carnival, when papier-mâché *gegants* (giants) totter among the laughing crowds; and, at the markets, the arrival of the first spring vegetables. The young produce is a colorful and wide-ranging bounty, with artichokes so tender they can be eaten raw (or sliced and cooked *a la planxa*); little white-and-purple turnips with bright green tops; the first asparagus from Aragón and Navarre; fresh garlic, sweet and mild enough to use with generous abandon; and, above all, the first baby beans and peas in their pods, much adored by the Catalans and celebrated in such dishes as *faves a la catalana* and *pèsols de llavaneres ofegats* (braised peas). When spring hits the city, there's no better way to exploit its gifts than with a grand platter of steamed fresh vegetables, simply dressed with butter and pepper or olive oil and lemon juice. Another favorite use for all these riches is a vegetable paella made with quartered artichokes, fava beans, peas, asparagus, Swiss chard stalks, baby turnips, and sliced garlic.

TRINXAT

Mashed Potatoes and Cabbage

Like many of the best-known Catalan dishes, this is a simple preparation. It consists of cooked cabbage and potatoes roughly mashed together and topped with fried strips of cansalada, *or cured pork fat (a flavorful, salty, unsmoked bacon is a good substitute).* Trinxat, *which means "mashed," is the kind of dish a farmer's wife might whip up at the end of a cold winter's day. Some say it tastes best after the first frost, which has the effect of improving the flavor of winter cabbage. Although its roots are in the Pyrenees, this dish is now found on the menus of many upscale restaurants. It is sometimes accompanied by* allioli *(page 105).*

Salt and freshly ground pepper

1 head green cabbage, about 1 lb (500 g), cored and sliced

1 lb (500 g) Yukon gold or other yellow-fleshed potatoes, cut into thick slices

½ lb (250 g) *cansalada, panceta,* or unsmoked bacon

¼ cup (2 fl oz/60 ml) olive oil

1 teaspoon pimentón or sweet paprika

1 clove garlic, minced

Makes 4 servings

1 Bring a large pot three-fourths full of water to a boil over high heat. Salt the water, add the cabbage, and cook until just tender, about 15 minutes. Add the potatoes and cook until tender when pierced with a knife, about 10 minutes longer. Drain the cabbage and potatoes, then transfer to a large bowl. Using a fork or a potato masher, roughly mash the cabbage and potatoes together. Transfer to a serving dish and season to taste with salt and pepper (be careful not to use too much salt—the bacon will be quite salty).

2 While the potatoes are cooking, fry the pork: Remove the skin or rind from the *cansalada, panceta,* or bacon and cut into ½-inch (12-mm) pieces. In a frying pan over medium-high heat, warm the olive oil. Add the pork pieces and fry until crisp, about 5 minutes. Using a slotted spoon, transfer the pieces to paper towels to drain, reserving the pan with the oil.

3 Away from the heat, add the pimentón and garlic to the reserved oil. Return to medium-high heat and sauté until the oil is colored and the garlic begins to brown, about 30 seconds. Pour the garlic oil over the potato-cabbage mixture. Scatter the pork pieces over the top and serve at once.

Serve with an intensely flavored, aromatic, silky red wine from Aragon.

CEPS AL FORN

Oven-Roasted Wild Mushrooms with Garlic and Parsley

Porcini, also known as ceps or cèpes, are the meatiest, juiciest, and most robustly flavored of all the wild mushrooms of autumn. They arrive in the markets of Barcelona at the beginning of October, after the first rains, and are eagerly snapped up. One of the best uses for this delicacy is also the simplest: oven roasted with a picada, the mixture of herbs, ground nuts, and spices often added to Catalan dishes. The following recipe was adapted from one by writer and gastronome Pep Palau, an acknowledged expert in Catalan mushroom cookery.

1 To clean the mushrooms, cut away the base of the stems and remove any dirt with a soft brush or a damp cloth (it is best not to wash them). Cut any large mushrooms in half or into pieces, leaving the smaller mushrooms whole.

2 In a dry frying pan over low heat, sweat the mushrooms to remove any excess moisture, about 5 minutes. Add the olive oil and season with salt and pepper. Raise the heat to medium-high and sauté, turning the mushrooms to coat all sides, for about 5 minutes. Remove from the heat and set aside.

3 Preheat the oven to 400°F (200°C). To make the *picada,* using a mortar and pestle, crush together the garlic and salt, then add the parsley and olive oil and grind until a thick, smooth paste forms, about 10 minutes. Add the bread crumbs and mix well.

4 Butter a roasting pan in which the mushrooms will fit in a single layer. Transfer the mushrooms to the pan and drizzle the *picada* over them. Roast until the mushrooms are sizzling, about 5 minutes. Turn on the broiler (grill) and broil (grill) until lightly browned, 1–2 minutes longer. Transfer to a warmed platter and serve at once.

Serve with a tannic, aromatic Spanish red wine.

1 lb (500 g) fresh porcini (cep) mushrooms

½ cup (4 fl oz/125 ml) extra-virgin olive oil

Salt and freshly ground pepper

FOR THE PICADA

2 cloves garlic, quartered

½ teaspoon salt

Handful of fresh flat-leaf (Italian) parsley leaves, roughly chopped

1 tablespoon extra-virgin olive oil

⅓ cup (½ oz/15 g) fresh bread crumbs

Makes 4 servings

Wild Mushrooms

The enthusiasm for wild mushrooms in Catalonia goes beyond logic and reason. Local gastronome Pep Palau chalks it up to something in the national Catalan character: a need to experience the authentic side of the culture. Whatever the explanation, the lower slopes of the Pyrenees, with their deciduous forests, are a paradise for mushroom hunters.

Mushroom hunting at its present level of intensity actually began no more than a decade or so ago. Llorenç Petràs, owner of the Petràs mushroom stall in La Boqueria market, and one of Catalonia's greatest authorities on fungi of all kinds, remembers that twenty years ago there was only one species the Catalans would touch: the *rovelló,* or *níscalo (Lactarius deliciosus),* known in English as the saffron milk cap. They were fearful of all the rest, which they cheerfully exchanged for coffee and sugar with their French neighbors across the Pyrenees. While *rovellons* are still a popular and sought-after species, the situation today is a very different story, and chanterelles, porcini (ceps), parasols, and at least a dozen other varieties are all highly popular

ESCALIVADA
Roasted Vegetable Salad

On summer weekends, Barcelona families like to repair to the wooded hills behind the city, where they fire up barbecues and while away the afternoon with food, wine, and naps in deck chairs. The menu on these occasions will often feature grilled lamb, pork, and botifarres *(sausages), as well as vegetables briefly grilled over the coals and combined to make* escalivada, *one of the Mediterranean's most original salads. It is another Catalan dish that is tied firmly to a particular season, in this case summer, when eggplants, bell peppers, and tomatoes are in abundance and at their best.*

4 red bell peppers (capsicums), about 2 lb (1 kg) total weight

2 large or 4 small eggplants (aubergines), about 2 lb (1 kg) total weight

2 yellow onions, unpeeled

4 tomatoes, about 1 lb (500 g) total weight

1 head garlic

Coarse salt

1 cup (8 fl oz/250 ml) olive oil

Extra-virgin olive oil for drizzling

3 tablespoons red wine vinegar

Makes 4 servings

1 Preheat the oven to 400°F (200°C). Place the bell peppers, eggplants, onions, tomatoes, and garlic in a single layer on a large baking sheet. Sprinkle with salt and pour the 1 cup olive oil evenly over the top. Roast the tomatoes until their skins have split and started to blacken, about 20 minutes. Using tongs, transfer the tomatoes to a bowl. Continue roasting the remaining vegetables, turning once, until the onions are soft and translucent and the skins of the eggplant and peppers are blistered and beginning to blacken, 25–40 minutes longer.

2 Remove the vegetables from the oven and let stand until cool enough to handle. Peel the bell peppers, then slice each pepper in half lengthwise and discard the seeds, ribs, and stems. Chop the peppers coarsely. Peel the eggplants and chop coarsely. Peel the onions and tomatoes and chop coarsely. Place the peppers, eggplants, onions, and tomatoes in a serving bowl. Separate the cloves of garlic and gently squeeze out the roasted flesh from each one. Add to the bowl with the vegetables.

3 Dress the salad with salt to taste, a drizzling of extra-virgin olive oil, and the vinegar. Toss the salad gently but thoroughly and serve warm.

Serve with a fresh, fruity rosé from Navarre.

CALÇOTADA

Grilled Green Onions with Romesco Sauce

On Saturdays and Sundays from February through April, the citizens of Barcelona jump into their cars and race down the motorways to restaurants specializing in calçotades. Originally from Valls, this specialty has rapidly become popular throughout the region. The season's first new green onions (calçots) are roasted over coals until the outer skins are blackened and the interiors are sweet and tender. Diners peel off the burned outer skins and dunk the onions into romesco sauce before eating them. It's a messy business requiring paper bibs.

1 To make the sauce, prepare a fire in a charcoal grill or preheat a gas grill on high. Grill the garlic, turning as needed, until browned on all sides, 13–15 minutes. Grill the tomatoes, turning once, until the skins are browned and wrinkled, about 5 minutes. Set aside and let cool.

2 Peel the garlic cloves. Using a large mortar and pestle, grind together the garlic and nuts. Peel the tomatoes and add to the mortar along with the baguette slices. Grind well until a thick paste forms. (Alternatively, place the peeled garlic and tomatoes, nuts, and baguette slices in a food processor and pulse to combine.) Mix in the ½ cup olive oil, 2 tablespoons vinegar, the pimentón, and salt to taste. The finished sauce should be thick but not dry; add more oil and vinegar if needed. Divide among individual dipping bowls and set aside. (The sauce will keep in an airtight container in the refrigerator for up to 5 days; bring to room temperature before serving.)

3 While you are making the sauce, place the onions on the grill and grill, turning occasionally, until the outer skins have blackened and shriveled, about 8 minutes. Wrap the onions in newspaper and let stand until cool enough to handle, about 5 minutes.

4 Transfer the onions to a large serving platter or a wooden board. Diners peel the onions with their fingers and dip each one into the *romesco* sauce. Serve with crusty bread.

Serve with a slightly chilled, young, light-bodied Rioja.

FOR THE SAUCE

1 head garlic

2 ripe tomatoes

¾ cup (4 oz/125 g) blanched almonds, toasted (page 109)

½ cup (2 oz/60 g) hazelnuts (filberts), toasted and skinned (page 178)

4 small baguette slices

½ cup (4 fl oz/125 ml) extra-virgin olive oil, or to taste

2 tablespoons red wine vinegar, or to taste

1 teaspoon pimentón or sweet paprika

Salt

24 green (spring) onions, each about 1 inch (2.5 cm) wide at the base and with plenty of white flesh

Crusty bread for serving

Makes 4 servings

Fiesta Foods: Calçots

Like the rest of the Iberian peninsula, Catalonia has its innumerable *festes*. But the food-related fiesta, or *aplec*—the celebration of an individual ingredient or dish—is particularly characteristic of the *països catalans*. In the last few years, such events have multiplied a hundred-fold, until it seems practically every town or village has its special day of tastings, feasting, and partying.

It started with the *calçotada*. *Calçots* are a type of green (spring) onion harvested between January and February. In the region of the Baix Camp outside of Tarragona (of which Valls is the capital), the onions have long been roasted over coals and served with a local version of *romesco* sauce. The idea of dipping them, caramelized from the fire, into this rich sauce is inspired and delicious. At Masia Bou, a farmhouse near Valls, the hosts found themselves serving *calçots* to parties of locals. The onions were only the first course, followed by barbecued meats, but they were greeted with so much excitement that the *calçotada* was born. The custom has spread from Valls into the rest of Catalonia.

AMANIDA CATALANA

Catalan Salad

The typical Spanish ensalada mixta, with its canned asparagus, grated carrot, and sweet corn, is a dreary dish—inexplicably so, given the enormous variety and quality of the salad ingredients grown in Spain. In Barcelona, you can easily avoid this typically unappetizing mixed salad by ordering the amanida catalana. This is one of the two national salads (the other is xató, page 109). It originated in the countryside, where it was brought to the workers at lunchtime during the summer wheat harvest. With its wealth of protein and bright colors, it must have come as a welcome sight after the heat and dust of the long morning's work.

FOR THE VINAIGRETTE

3 tablespoons red wine vinegar

Salt and freshly ground pepper

½ cup (4 fl oz/125 ml) extra-virgin olive oil

2 ripe tomatoes

2 hard-boiled eggs, peeled

8 cups (10 oz/315 g) torn mixed salad greens such as romaine (cos) lettuce, escarole (Batavian endive), and chicory (curly endive)

1 red onion, cut into thin rings

1 green bell pepper (capsicum), seeded and cut into narrow strips

6 olive oil–packed anchovy fillets

12 oil-cured black olives

4 thin slices serrano ham or prosciutto

16–20 thin slices cured sausage such as *salchichón*, salami, chorizo, or *sobrassada*

Makes 4 servings

1 To make the vinaigrette, in a bowl, whisk together the vinegar and ½ teapoon salt. Slowly add the olive oil while whisking constantly. Taste and adjust the seasoning with salt and pepper.

2 Quarter the tomatoes and eggs lengthwise and place them in a large bowl with the salad greens. Add the onion and bell pepper and toss together along with the vinaigrette to mix evenly.

3 Pile the mixture on a large serving platter and decorate with the anchovies and olives. Cut the ham slices into 3-inch squares. Arrange the sliced ham and sausages around the platter. Serve at once.

Serve with a jug of sangria.

CREMA DE LLENTIES

Cream of Lentil Soup with Garlic-Herb Croutons

Cal Isidre, an esteemed, family-run eatery on the Carrer Les Flors, specializes in Catalan cuisine made with luxury ingredients and enormous dedication. The lentil soup is a revelation. Puréeing the humble lentil seems to transform it completely. By nature earthy and rustic, it becomes velvety and voluptuous, like a country bumpkin magically transformed into an aristocrat. At Cal Isidre, this soup is served with a garnish of fried cansalada *(cured pork fat) and* botifarra negra *(blood sausage). In this version, the blood sausage has been replaced with crisp croutons flavored with garlic and fresh herbs.*

1 To make the soup, in a saucepan over medium-high heat, combine the mineral water, lentils, half-and-half, butter, and ham bone. Bring to a boil, reduce the heat to medium-low, cover partially, and simmer gently until the lentils are soft but not disintegrating, about 40 minutes.

2 Discard the ham bone. In a food processor or blender, working in batches if necessary, process the lentils until smooth. Strain the purée through a fine-mesh sieve. (The goal of both puréeing and straining is to reach a perfectly creamy consistency.) Return the purée to the saucepan and season to taste with salt and pepper. Cover and keep warm over low heat.

3 To make the topping, in a small, heavy frying pan over medium heat, warm the olive oil. Add the bacon and fry until crisp, about 6 minutes. Using a slotted spoon, transfer the bacon to paper towels to drain. Add the garlic to the oil in the pan and sauté until translucent, about 2 minutes. Add the bread cubes and sauté until both the garlic and bread are golden brown, about 3 minutes longer. Using a slotted spoon, transfer the croutons and garlic to paper towels to drain. In a bowl, combine the croutons and garlic with the bacon. Add the chopped herbs and toss gently to combine.

4 Ladle the soup into warmed individual bowls and top each serving with one-fourth of the crouton mixture. Serve at once.

Serve with a light, intensely colored young red wine such as Rioja.

FOR THE SOUP

4 cups (32 fl oz/1 l) still mineral water

1½ cups (10½ oz/330 g) small green lentils, such as Puy lentils, rinsed

1 cup (8 fl oz/250 ml) half-and-half (half cream)

1 tablespoon unsalted butter

1 ham bone, about 6 oz (185 g)

Salt and freshly ground pepper

FOR THE TOPPING

¼ cup (2 fl oz/60 ml) extra-virgin olive oil

¼ lb (125 g) bacon, chopped

3 cloves garlic, thinly sliced

2 thick slices coarse country white bread, about 3 oz (90 g) total weight, crusts removed and bread cut into 1-inch (2.5-cm) cubes

Handful of mixed fresh herb leaves, such as chervil, flat-leaf (Italian) parsley, chives, and tarragon, finely chopped

Makes 4 servings

TRUITA AMB SUC

Spinach Omelet with Tomato Sauce

This is a variation of the traditional Spanish tortilla, *unusual because the omelet is finished in a rich tomato and garlic sauce (called* suc *in Catalan) in a terra-cotta dish. Once a year, the inhabitants of Ulldemolins, a town in the Priorat—one of the most beautiful wine-growing areas in the world—hold a celebration of the* truita amb suc, *with demonstrations and tastings. Each cook brings his or her own version of the dish. Classically, the omelet contains spinach and sometimes potato, but other vegetables are often added, too. A mixture of ground nuts and parsley, or* picada, *gives an authentically Catalan finish to the dish.*

2 lb (1 kg) fresh spinach, stemmed, or 1 package (14 oz/440 g) frozen spinach, thawed

½ cup (4 fl oz/125 ml) plus 2 tablespoons olive oil

6 large eggs

Salt and freshly ground pepper

8 cloves garlic, minced

1 tablespoon all-purpose (plain) flour

2 cups (16 fl oz/500 ml) tomato purée

1 teaspoon pimentón or sweet paprika

1 cup (8 fl oz/250 ml) hot water

FOR THE PICADA

12 blanched almonds

1 tablespoon extra-virgin olive oil

1 slice coarse country white bread, about 1 oz (30 g), crust removed

Handful of fresh flat-leaf (Italian) parsley leaves

Crusty country bread for serving

Makes 6 servings

1 If using fresh spinach, put the spinach with just the rinsing water clinging to the leaves in a saucepan over medium-high heat, cover, and cook until the spinach is bright green and wilted, about 2 minutes. Remove from the heat and drain well in a sieve, pressing the spinach with the back of a spoon to remove excess moisture. When the spinach is cool, chop it coarsely and set aside. If using frozen spinach, drain well, pressing out all excess moisture.

2 In a wide, heavy, shallow frying pan over medium heat, warm the ½ cup olive oil. Add the spinach and sauté until hot, about 2 minutes.

3 In a large bowl, beat the eggs until blended. Transfer the spinach to the bowl with the eggs and mix evenly. Season with salt and pepper. Reserve the pan with the remaining oil.

4 Return the pan containing the oil to medium heat. Gently pour the egg and spinach mixture into the pan and cook until the bottom of the omelet is golden, about 5 minutes (use a spatula to lift the edge of the omelet to check for doneness). Remove the pan from the heat. Invert a plate on top of the pan and carefully invert the pan and plate together. Lift off the pan, letting the omelet fall onto the plate. Slide the omelet back into the pan to brown the other side, about 3 minutes longer. (If the egg mixture has stuck to the pan, brown the top under the broiler/grill instead.)

5 In a *cassola* or flameproof ceramic baking dish over medium heat, warm the remaining 2 tablespoons olive oil. Add the garlic and sauté until golden,

about 2 minutes. Remove from the heat and add the flour. Return to the heat and cook, stirring constantly, until the mixture is smooth and creamy, 1–2 minutes. Add the tomato purée, pimentón, hot water, and salt to taste. Cook, stirring, until the sauce is reduced slightly but not too thick, about 5 minutes.

6 Cut the omelet into 6 pieces and slide the pieces into the *cassola* with the sauce so that the sauce almost covers them. After 15 minutes of bubbling— what the Catalans call *xup-xup*—turn off the heat.

7 To make the *picada,* in a dry frying pan over high heat, toast the almonds until golden brown, about 2 minutes. Transfer to a plate to cool. In the same pan over medium heat, warm the olive oil. Add the bread and fry on both sides until crisp, about 2 minutes on each side. Using a mortar and pestle, grind together the toasted almonds, fried bread, and parsley.

8 Transfer the omelet pieces to individual plates, top with some of the sauce, and sprinkle the *picada* on top. Serve at room temperature with plenty of crusty country bread for mopping up the sauce.

Serve with a straw-colored, herbaceous white wine from the Priorat.

CANELONS DE FESTA

Feast-Day Cannelloni

For centuries, Barcelona has maintained ties with Italy. As Colman Andrews explains in Catalan Cuisine, the influx of Italian restaurateurs in the nineteenth century brought a number of formerly unfamiliar ingredients. Even today, many visitors are surprised at just how much pasta is consumed in Barcelona. Canelons—cannelloni stuffed with mixed meats and served with a thick béchamel—are traditionally served on holidays. In fact, if the city had a signature dish, it would probably be the rich and comforting canelons de festa.

1 Bring a pot three-fourths full of water to a boil. Salt the water, add the pasta, and cook until al dente, 10–12 minutes. Drain and lay out on paper towels.

2 To make the béchamel, in a heavy-bottomed saucepan over low heat, melt the butter. Remove the pan from the heat, sprinkle in the flour, and whisk to combine. Return to the heat and cook 2–3 minutes, stirring constantly. Add the milk little by little, whisking constantly to prevent lumps. Reduce the heat to low and cook, stirring, until the sauce coats the back of a spoon, 3–5 minutes. Season to taste with salt and pepper and add the nutmeg. Set aside and keep warm.

3 Preheat the oven to 425°F (220°C). Grease a 9-by-12-inch (23-by-30-cm) baking dish. In a frying pan over medium heat, warm the olive oil. Add the onion and garlic and sauté until softened, 3–4 minutes. Add the ham, chicken, and pork and sauté until cooked through, 5–6 minutes. Add the bread crumbs and livers and sauté 1–2 minutes. Add the wine, season with salt and pepper, stir, and cook until the wine reduces, about 4 minutes. Remove from the heat and stir in the yolks.

4 Spread 1 tablespoon filling down the middle of each pasta square. Roll into tubes and lay them, seam side down and side by side, in the prepared dish.

5 Whisk three-fourths of the cheese into the sauce and pour over the cannelloni. Sprinkle with the rest of the cheese and dot the surface with the butter. Bake until golden brown and bubbling, about 15 minutes.

Serve with a rich, berry-tasting red wine from Cigales.

Salt and freshly ground pepper

1 package (about 1 lb/500 g) dried cannelloni or lasagna squares

FOR THE BÉCHAMEL

¼ cup (2 oz/60 g) unsalted butter

⅓ cup (2 oz/60 g) all-purpose (plain) flour

2 cups (16 fl oz/500 ml) whole milk

Pinch of freshly grated nutmeg

¼ cup (2 fl oz/60 ml) olive oil

1 yellow onion, finely chopped

6 cloves garlic, minced

2 oz (60 g) serrano ham, shredded

½ lb (250 g) *each* ground (minced) chicken and pork

1 cup (2 oz/60 g) fresh bread crumbs

¼ lb (125 g) chicken livers, trimmed and ground (minced)

⅓ cup (3 fl oz/80 ml) *vi ranci*, sweet sherry, or vermouth

2 egg yolks, lightly beaten

5 oz (155 g) cured Mahón or Parmesan cheese, grated

1 tablespoon unsalted butter

Makes 6 servings

Italian Influences

For long periods of its history, Catalonia had more cultural contact with Italy than with the rest of Spain. As an important seaport, Barcelona maintained trade links with Italy, particularly Genoa, absorbing many Italian customs and an appreciation of the Italian aesthetic at the same time. At the end of the eighteenth century, Italian restaurateurs in Barcelona began to make foods such as spaghetti, macaroni, and saltimbocca commonplace. One of the best-loved dishes in the city uses macaroni and is called *macarrons a la catalana*. It is served *a la cassola* (in a ceramic baking dish) with a sauce of ground roasted meat, tomato, and grated Mahón cheese. These days, Italian cuisine in the form of pizza, pasta, and so on is as prominent in Barcelona as in any other world city, and Italian terms such as carpaccio, risotto, and *semifreddo* have begun to appear on the menus of the city's most creative restaurants. A great contribution to authentic Italian food is the pastas and ice creams produced by Sandro Desii in Esparreguera, outside Barcelona. His *fideos* and other hand-made pastas are decidedly the equal of anything made in his homeland.

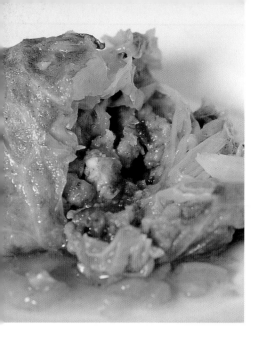

FARCELLETS DE COL
Pork and Cabbage Bundles

The idea of wrapping minced meat in leaves and braising the bundles in a small amount of liquid is not unique to Catalan cooking. The Greeks and Turks are fond of using vine leaves for their dolmades. The Romanian sarmale, *ground meat wrapped in cabbage leaves, is an Easter specialty similar to* farcellets. *The success of these latter dishes depends on using the correct kind of cabbage: a large head with thick, loose leaves (savoy is ideal), rather than a variety with tightly packed leaves that tear easily. Served with steamed rice or crusty bread to mop up the juices,* farcellets *make a hearty autumn dish.*

16 large cabbage leaves, preferably savoy

Salt and freshly ground pepper

FOR THE SOFREGIT

⅓ cup (3 fl oz/80 ml) olive oil

2 yellow onions, finely chopped

1 carrot, peeled and finely chopped

6 cloves garlic, finely chopped

FOR THE FILLING

10 oz (315 g) ground (minced) lean pork

10 oz (315 g) ground (minced) veal or beef

Salt and freshly ground pepper

1 large egg, lightly beaten

All-purpose (plain) flour for dusting

2 tablespoons olive oil or lard

½ cup (4 fl oz/125 ml) dry white wine

½ cup (4 fl oz/125 ml) beef, chicken, or vegetable stock or water

Makes 6–8 servings

1 Trim the tough stalk at the end of the cabbage leaves. Pour water to a depth of 1 inch (2.5 cm) into a wide, shallow pan with a tight-fitting lid. Bring to a boil over medium heat, then add a large pinch of salt. Lay the cabbage leaves in the pan, cover, and simmer just until tender, about 10 minutes. Using tongs, transfer the leaves to paper towels to drain.

2 Preheat the oven to 350°F (180°C). To make a *sofregit,* in a frying pan over medium heat, warm the olive oil. Add the onions, carrot, and garlic and sauté until the onions are softened, about 6 minutes. Spread half of the *sofregit* mixture in the bottom of a *cassola* or shallow ceramic baking dish.

3 To make the filling, add the pork and veal to the pan with the remaining *sofregit* mixture and cook together until the meat is lightly browned, about 8 minutes. Transfer the meat to a bowl, season well with salt and pepper, and stir in the egg.

4 Place a heaping tablespoonful of the filling in the center of each cabbage leaf. For each leaf, fold the sides of the leaf over the filling, then roll into a neat parcel roughly the size of a large egg. Seal each *farcellet* with a toothpick.

5 Dust the *farcellets* with flour. In a wide, heavy-bottomed frying pan over medium-high heat, warm the olive oil. In batches, add the *farcellets* and fry on all sides until golden brown, about 5 minutes. As you finish frying the *farcellets,* arrange them in the *cassola* on top of the *sofregit.* When all the bundles are cooked, deglaze the frying pan with the wine, scraping to stir up any browned bits. Stir in the stock and then pour the contents of the pan over the *farcellets.*

6 Cover the *cassola* and bake the *farcellets* until cooked through, about 30 minutes. Let cool for a few minutes before serving.

Serve with a full-bodied Merlot or Cabernet Sauvignon from the Alella region.

SEGONS PLATS

Steeped in tradition, hearty dishes such as *fideuà*, whole fish baked in salt,

braised beef, and roasted garlic chicken are staples of the Catalan diet.

Almost every town in Catalonia contributes to the splendid variety of food in the region, from the generously flavored rice dishes of the south and the fish soups and *suquets* of the north to the game stews of the Pyrenees and the grilled meats popular all over the country. Vegetables are an integral part of the Barcelona menu and are incorporated into most classic main courses. With rustic dishes like *pollastre rostit* (roasted chicken) and *civet de senglar* (wild boar stew), first courses can be dispensed with if you are generous with the appetizers. A simple green salad served with the *segon plat* may be all these dishes need for accompaniment.

PAELLA PARELLADA

Shellfish and Mixed Meat Paella

The name Parellada crops up regularly in Catalan food lore, partly thanks to Ramón and Ada Parellada, two pillars of the Barcelona restaurant scene, and partly due to their father, Paco, who owned the venerable Set Portes restaurant, which was originally founded in 1836 and still one of the city's most popular eating places. In the 1940s, Senyor Parellada began serving the paella Parellada at Set Portes. The dish has since become the restaurant's house specialty and a classic of Barcelona eating. Though originally from Valencia, paella has spread all around the Spanish Mediterranean, with every region boasting its own version.

1 In a saucepan over medium heat, bring the stock to a gentle simmer and maintain over low heat.

2 To prepare the artichokes, fill a bowl with water and stir in the lemon juice. Working with 1 artichoke at a time, remove the tough outer leaves. Slice off the top 2 inches (5 cm) of the remaining leaves. Cut the stem off flush with the base and discard. Cut the artichoke lengthwise into quarters, then scrape out and discard the fuzzy choke with a spoon or a small, sharp knife. Place the cleaned artichoke quarters in the lemon water. Repeat with the remaining artichokes.

3 Using a mortar and pestle, grind 1 teaspoon salt with the saffron until a powder forms. Add the garlic and grind with the salt and saffron. Set aside. Cut the chicken thigh meat, pork loin, and sausages into 1-inch (2.5-cm) pieces. Slice the squid into rings, leaving the tentacles whole.

4 Place a 16-inch (40-cm) paella pan or a large, wide, heavy-bottomed frying pan over high heat (or over a metal ring set on a rack over coals) and add the olive oil. When the oil is hot, add the chicken, pork, squid, and sausages and sauté until golden, about 10 minutes. Transfer the meat and seafood to a plate with a slotted spoon and set aside. Reserve the pan with the remaining oil.

5 Drain the artichokes and add to the paella pan. Add the onion and bell pepper and sauté over medium heat until the onion is translucent and beginning to brown, about 3 minutes. Return the meat and squid to the pan and add the tomatoes,

stirring so that the tomatoes are evenly distributed. Add 2 ladlefuls of the hot stock and allow to simmer for 1–2 minutes.

6 Stir a little stock into the mortar with the saffron mixture and mix well. Pour the contents of the mortar into the saucepan of stock.

7 Add the rice to the meat and vegetables in the paella pan, followed by the peas and all but ½ cup (4 fl oz/125 ml) of the remaining stock. Stir everything together thoroughly.

8 Cut the monkfish into 1-inch (2.5-cm) pieces. Scrub the mussels with a stiff brush. Debeard them by scraping the tuft of fibers off with a knife. Remove them from their shells if desired. Arrange the fish, mussels, and shrimp on top of the rice mixture, discarding any mussels that do not close to the touch. Return the paella to a simmer and cook until the meat and fish are cooked through and the rice is tender but not too soft, about 20 minutes. If mussels are in their shells, discard any that failed to open. If the paella is not yet done and all the liquid is absorbed, add a little of the reserved stock as needed.

9 Turn off the heat and cover the pan with a clean dry kitchen towel. Let stand for about 10 minutes to allow the flavors to mingle thoroughly and the rice to absorb any remaining juices. Serve warm, not hot, garnished with the parsley.

Serve with a juicy, fresh young white wine such as Rueda or Verdejo.

4 cups (32 fl oz/1 l) chicken stock

Juice of ½ lemon

4 large artichokes

Coarse sea salt

1 teaspoon saffron threads

3 cloves garlic, thinly sliced

6 chicken thighs, boned

⅓ lb (155 g) pork loin

½ lb (250 g) pork sausages

7 oz (220 g) cleaned squid

1 cup (8 fl oz/250 ml) olive oil

1 yellow onion, thinly sliced

1 red bell pepper (capsicum), seeded and cut into 1-inch (2.5-cm) pieces

1 lb (500 g) ripe tomatoes, peeled, seeded (page 187), and finely chopped

2½ cups (1 lb/500 g) risotto-type short-grain rice such as Bomba

1 cup (5 oz/155 g) shelled English peas, fresh or frozen

6 oz (185 g) monkfish or hake fillet

24 large mussels

12 medium shrimp (prawns), peeled

Fresh flat-leaf (Italian) parsley

Makes 8 servings

FRICANDÓ AMB MOIXERNONS
Braised Beef with Mushrooms

The mushrooms most commonly used for fricandó, *a rich, dark, and flavorful beef stew, are* moixernons, *which are small and unassuming to look at but give off a heavenly aroma. They are sold at Llorenç Petràs's mushroom stall at Barcelona's La Boqueria market (page 25), and elsewhere in Catalonia, and can be bought dried from mail-order and online sources (page 187). Left to soak overnight, they will perfume your kitchen with a fragrance of autumn woods and damp earth. If* moixernons *are unavailable, substitute any flavorful wild mushrooms.* Fricandó *is traditionally served with sautéed potatoes.*

1 cup (5 oz/ 155 g) all-purpose (plain) flour

Salt and freshly ground pepper

2 lb (1 kg) beef rump roast, chuck roast, or skirt steak, cut into slices ½ inch (12 mm) thick

⅓ cup (3 fl oz/80 ml) olive oil

2 *each* fresh oregano, thyme, and marjoram sprigs or 1 teaspoon *each* dried oregano, thyme, and marjoram

1 fresh rosemary sprig or ½ teaspoon dried rosemary

2 yellow onions, thinly sliced

2 tomatoes, cored

3 cloves garlic, crushed

1 cup (8 fl oz/250 ml) dry white wine

1 bay leaf

2 pinches of freshly grated nutmeg

1 oz (30 g) bittersweet chocolate

2 oz (60 g) dried wild mushrooms, soaked in water to cover overnight

3 cups (24 fl oz/750 ml) beef stock

Makes 6 servings

1 Place the flour in a shallow bowl, season with salt and pepper, and stir to combine. Lightly dredge the beef slices on both sides in the seasoned flour, shaking off any excess.

2 In a heavy-bottomed Dutch oven or flameproof ceramic baking dish over medium heat, warm the olive oil. Working in batches if necessary, add the beef and brown on all sides, about 5 minutes. Transfer the beef to a plate with a slotted spoon. Reserve the pot with the remaining oil.

3 Next, make a *sofregit*. If using fresh oregano, thyme, marjoram, and rosemary sprigs, tie them in a bundle with kitchen string and set aside. Return the pot to medium heat, add the onions, and sauté until soft, about 3 minutes. Cut the tomatoes in half and, using the large holes of a grater-shredder, grate the pulp directly into the pot. Discard the skins. Add the garlic. When the vegetables are cooked, after about 4 minutes, add the wine. Add the herb bundle

or dried herbs and the bay leaf and nutmeg. Then grate the chocolate directly into the pot. Simmer over medium heat until the ingredients begin to form a sauce, about 5 minutes.

4 Drain the mushrooms in a sieve lined with cheesecloth (muslin), reserving the liquid, and add to the pot. Return the beef to the pot with any juices. Add the stock and enough of the mushroom-soaking liquid to cover the beef. Season to taste with salt and pepper.

5 Reduce the heat to low, cover partially, and cook until the beef is thoroughly tender and the sauce is thick and concentrated, about 1 hour. If using fresh herbs, remove and discard the herb bundle, and then discard the bay leaf. Transfer to a warmed serving dish or serve in the Dutch oven.

Serve with a rich, beefy, tannic red wine from the Montsant or Priorat.

BACALLÀ AMB SAMFAINA

Salt Cod with Eggplant, Peppers, Onion, and Tomato

Salt cod is one of the staple foods of Catalonia, and serving it in samfaina *is one of the most popular ways of preparing it. Samfaina is reminiscent of French ratatouille, a simple stew of Mediterranean summer vegetables such as eggplant, peppers, onions, and tomatoes, although in Catalonia it is considered a sauce rather than something to be eaten on its own. The slight sweetness of the vegetables balances the saltiness of the cod. Bacallà amb samfaina needs no accompaniment other than a basket of good crusty bread.*

1 To prepare the salt cod, place it in a large bowl of cold water, cover, and refrigerate for 3 days, changing the water 3 times.

2 To make the *samfaina,* sprinkle the eggplant with salt and let drain in a colander set over a bowl for about 1 hour. Rinse and thoroughly dry. Meanwhile, place the tomatoes in a food processor or blender and purée. Set aside.

3 In a large frying pan over medium heat, warm the ½ cup olive oil. Add the eggplant, onion, and bell peppers and cook gently until the vegetables are soft, about 5 minutes. Stir in the tomato purée and season with a generous grinding of pepper. (Do not add salt, as the cod will properly season the dish while cooking.) Cook, stirring occasionally, until thickened, about 20 minutes. Remove from the heat, cover, and set aside.

4 Drain the salt cod, remove any bones or skin, and cut into 3-inch (7.5-cm) chunks. Dust with flour. In a wide saucepan over medium-high heat, warm the 2 tablespoons olive oil. Add the cod and sauté gently, moving the pieces as little as possible to keep them whole, until lightly browned, 5 minutes.

5 Transfer the cod pieces to the frying pan so that each piece is surrounded by sauce. Place over low heat, cover, and cook until the sauce is bubbling around the fish, about 10 minutes. Sprinkle with the parsley and let cool slightly before serving.

Serve with a rich, well-balanced Spanish red wine.

1½ lb (750 g) salt cod

FOR THE SAMFAINA

1 large or 2 small eggplants (aubergines), cut into ½-inch (12-mm) dice

Salt and freshly ground pepper

3 or 4 large, ripe tomatoes, about 1 lb (500 g) total weight, peeled and seeded (page 187)

½ cup (4 fl oz/125 ml) olive oil

1 large yellow onion, cut into ½-inch (12-mm) dice

1 red bell pepper (capsicum), seeded and cut into ½-inch (12-mm) dice

1 green bell pepper (capsicum), seeded and cut into ½-inch (12-mm) dice

All-purpose (plain) flour for dusting

2 tablespoons olive oil

Leaves from 6 fresh flat-leaf (Italian) parsley sprigs, minced

Makes 4–6 servings

La Casa del Bacallà

Salt cod is old-fashioned, frugal food. In central Spain, in the days before refrigerators, it served to satisfy the demand for seafood, as the salting process allowed the fish to be kept almost indefinitely. *Bacallà a la llauna,* salt cod oven roasted with olive oil in a special tin plate, called a *llauna,* is often cited as the signature dish of Barcelona, although it is not often seen on restaurant menus nowadays. *Bacallà amb samfaina,* with the typical Catalan sauce of eggplant, bell peppers, onion, and tomato, is still a popular dish all over the region. Salt cod appears in many other dishes as well, from *esqueixada* (shredded in a salad) to *bunyols* (savory fritters) to *coques.*

La Casa del Bacallà is part of a nationwide chain that sells only cod from the Faroe Islands, regarded as the finest. Various cuts are available, from *morro* or *lomo* (the fattest and leanest, good for roasting) to *ventresca* (belly), *kokotxa* (cheeks), and *desmigado* (broken into small chunks). The fish must be desalted before use, typically by soaking it in plenty of cold water that is changed daily over three or four days.

CALDERETA DE LLAGOSTA
Lobster Soup

The little port of Fornells, on Minorca's rocky north coast, has set itself up as the capital of calldereta. King Juan Carlos has even been known to drop in at Es Plà, the most famous restaurant in town, when sailing past on his yacht. The calldereta *is a classically Mediterranean lobster dish, featuring peppers, tomatoes, garlic, and parsley. Spiny lobsters, a species without claws, are the traditional crustaceans used in this dish, but "true" lobsters will also do here. They must be live, however, as lobster meat deteriorates rapidly. When purchasing, look for a lively lobster that is heavy for its size and also has a hard shell.*

4 small live lobsters, about
1 lb (500 g) each

1 bay leaf

6 peppercorns

⅓ cup (3 fl oz/80 ml) olive oil

1 yellow onion, minced

1 red or green bell pepper
(capsicum), seeded and chopped

1 large ripe tomato, peeled,
seeded (page 187), and chopped

1 celery stalk, chopped

3 cloves garlic, minced

¼ cup fresh flat-leaf (Italian)
parsley sprigs, minced

Salt

4 slices coarse country bread,
about 4 oz (125 g) total
weight, toasted

Makes 4 servings

1 Bring a large pot three-fourths full of water to a boil over high heat. Immerse the live lobsters in the water and leave for 2 minutes, just long enough to kill them. Lift out with tongs and set on a work surface. When cool enough to handle, using a small, sharp knife, make a lengthwise cut along the underside of each lobster. Remove and discard the small intestine in the center of the tail. Detach and reserve the heads and legs, then cut each lobster crosswise into 4–6 pieces. Using a lobster cracker or mallet, gently crack the claws, if using "true" lobsters.

2 Remove the sand sac from the lobster head. If desired, scoop the creamy coral out of the heads, scramble with a fork in a small bowl, and set aside.

3 Use the reserved heads and legs to make the lobster stock: Place them in a saucepan with 5 cups (40 fl oz/1.25 l) water, the bay leaf, and the peppercorns and bring to a boil over high heat. Reduce the heat to medium and simmer about 15 minutes.

4 In a *cassola* or heavy flameproof ceramic baking dish over medium heat, warm the olive oil. Add the onion, bell pepper, tomato, celery, garlic, and parsley and sauté until the onion is softened, about 5 minutes. Stir in the reserved lobster coral, then add the lobster pieces, turning them so that they are well coated.

5 Strain the lobster stock through a colander or sieve lined with cheesecloth (muslin), discarding the heads and legs, the bay leaf, and the peppercorns. Add 4 cups (32 fl oz/1 l) of the stock to the *cassola* and bring to a boil over high heat. Reduce the heat to medium and cook until the meat turns opaque, about 10 minutes. Season to taste with salt.

6 To serve, place a slice of toast in each shallow soup bowl, and divide the lobster pieces evenly among them. Ladle the stock and vegetables over the top and serve at once.

Serve with a rich, full-bodied, oak-aged Spanish Chardonnay from the Penedès.

ARRÒS AMB CROSTA

Baked Rice with Chicken, Sausage, and Chickpeas

The town of Elche, in the southern part of the Catalan-speaking region, is famous for three very disparate things: the Dama de Elche, an ancient sculpture of a female figure; the Misteri de Elx, a religious drama enacted once a year in the town church; and the spectacular grove of palm trees that dates back to the presence of the Moors during the Middle Ages. Elche has a fourth claim to fame: this signature dish, a kind of paella of mixed meats and rice with a thin crust of beaten egg. It is delicious and lovely to look at, emerging from the oven with a golden yellow crust puffed up slightly around the meat, bean, and rice filling.

1 To make the stock, tie up the herb sprigs and bay leaf in a square of cheesecloth (muslin) with kitchen string and place in a large, heavy-bottomed stockpot with 4 cups (32 fl oz/1 l) water, the turnip, carrot, and onion. Bring to a boil over high heat. Reduce the heat to medium and simmer, uncovered, for 20 minutes.

2 In a bowl, mix the pork with the fresh bread crumbs and season well with salt and pepper. Form into balls about the size of small walnuts, and roll the meatballs in the dried bread crumbs. Set aside.

3 Cut each chicken thigh into 2 pieces. Season the rabbit and chicken pieces with salt and pepper. In a *cassola,* a flameproof ceramic baking dish, or a Dutch oven over medium heat, warm the ½ cup olive oil. Add the rabbit and chicken and sauté, turning as needed, until browned on all sides, about 6 minutes. Using a slotted spoon, transfer to the stockpot, reserving the remaining oil in the *cassola.*

4 Cut the pork sausages into 2-inch (5-cm) pieces. Return the *cassola* to medium heat and fry the sausage pieces until nicely browned, about 4 minutes. Using the slotted spoon, transfer to paper towels to drain, reserving the remaining oil in the *cassola.*

5 In a separate frying pan over medium heat, warm the 2 tablespoons oil. Add the meatballs and fry, turning, until golden brown, about 5 minutes. Using the slotted spoon, transfer to paper towels to drain.

6 Using a mortar and pestle, grind 1 teaspoon salt with the saffron threads until a deep yellow powder forms. Add the parsley and grind together to form a thick paste. Set aside.

7 Preheat the oven to 425°F (220°C). Return the *cassola* and oil to medium-high heat, add the garlic, and sauté until soft, about 2 minutes. (This may seem a large amount of garlic, but it is used only to flavor the oil.) Using the slotted spoon, remove the garlic from the pan and discard. Add the rice and sauté in the hot oil for about 30 seconds, then add the tomato and stir together for 30 seconds longer. Add 3 cups (24 fl oz/ 750 ml) of the stock, the rabbit and chicken pieces, and the sausage, then stir in the saffron-parsley mixture. Cook without stirring until all the liquid is absorbed, 12–15 minutes. Test the rice; the grains should be tender but not entirely soft. If further cooking is necessary, add a little more stock as needed. Remove from the heat and arrange the chickpeas and meatballs on top of the rice.

8 In a small bowl, beat the eggs with a whisk and pour them evenly over the rice. Immediately transfer to the oven and bake until the egg crust is opaque and beginning to brown, about 10 minutes. Remove from the oven and let cool slightly before serving.

Serve with a robust, full-bodied red wine from the Alicante.

---

6 mixed fresh herb sprigs such as thyme, oregano, and rosemary

1 bay leaf

1 *each* turnip, carrot, and small yellow onion, peeled and chopped

6 oz (185 g) ground (minced) pork

1 cup (2 oz/60 g) fresh bread crumbs

Sea salt and freshly ground pepper

½ cup (2 oz/60 g) dried bread crumbs

2 *each* chicken thighs and rabbit or chicken legs

½ cup (4 fl oz/125 ml) olive oil, plus 2 tablespoons

⅓ lb (155 g) pork sausages

1 teaspoon saffron threads

Leaves from 3 fresh flat-leaf (Italian) parsley sprigs

6 cloves garlic, coarsely chopped

1⅓ cups (9 oz/280 g) risotto-type short-grain rice such as Bomba

1 large tomato, peeled and chopped

¾ cup (5 oz/155 g) drained, canned chickpeas (garbanzo beans)

4 large eggs

Makes 4 servings

POLLASTRE ROSTIT
Roast Chicken with Garlic

Catalan cooks have always known the value of a fine roasting chicken. The region even has its own Denominació d'Origen for chickens, called Pollastre del Prat. The most popular method of cooking chicken is either with a samfaina (page 141) or grilled over a charcoal fire, closely followed by roasting in a terracotta cassola. The classic Mediterranean combination of garlic, tomatoes, herbs, and wine fills the kitchen with glorious aromas as the chicken browns and sizzles. Although the preparation is essentially simple, it is truly a dish for special occasions—what the Catalans call un plat de festa.

1 roasting chicken, preferably free-range, about 3 lb (1.5 kg), cut into 8 serving pieces

Salt and freshly ground pepper

¼ cup (2 oz/60 g) lard (optional)

¼ cup (2 fl oz/60 ml) olive oil

8 cloves garlic, peeled

1 cup (8 fl oz/250 ml) *vi ranci*, sweet sherry, or vermouth

2 yellow onions, cut into thick chunks

2 fresh oregano sprigs

2 bay leaves

4 small, ripe tomatoes, about 6 oz (185 g) total weight

Makes 4 servings

1 Preheat the oven to 350°F (180°C). Generously season the chicken pieces all over with salt and pepper. In a heavy frying pan over medium heat, melt the lard, if using, with the olive oil. Add the chicken pieces and cook, turning as needed, until golden brown on all sides, about 6 minutes. Add the garlic and cook for about 1 minute longer, then pour in the wine. Remove from the heat.

2 Distribute the onions in the bottom of a *cassola*, an ovenproof ceramic baking dish, or a Dutch oven about 10 inches (25 cm) in diameter. Arrange the chicken pieces on top of the onions. Shred the oregano and bay leaves over the chicken. Prick the tomatoes once or twice with the point of a sharp knife and place them among the chicken pieces. (The tomato juices will seep out as they cook, contributing to the sauce that forms at the bottom of the *cassola*.) Pour over the pan juices and the garlic.

3 Roast, turning the chicken pieces once or twice so that they brown evenly, until the meat is evenly browned and the skin is crispy, 45–60 minutes. Serve warm from the *cassola* or transfer to a serving platter.

Serve with a dry sparkling wine such as *cava* from Juvé i Camps, Codorníu, or Agustí Torelló.

POLLASTRE AMB GAMBES

Braised Chicken with Shrimp

Barcelona food is full of surprises. Visitors may find the combinations of fish and meat strange, with such mixtures as snails and pig's feet bordering on the surreal. But such dishes are not unusual even on the daily menu at unassuming places such as Barcelona's El Celler Vell, a homey lunch spot where this classic shrimp and chicken dish is offered. In its home-town of Tossa de Mar, a fishing village turned resort on the Costa Brava, the shrimp are sometimes replaced by lobster. In either case, it is a luxurious pairing.

1 Place the flour in a shallow bowl, season with salt and pepper, and stir to combine. Toss the chicken pieces in the flour, shaking off any excess.

2 In a large frying pan over medium heat, warm 2 tablespoons of the olive oil. Add the chicken pieces and cook, turning as needed, until golden brown on all sides, about 10 minutes. Using a slotted spoon, transfer the chicken to a flameproof ceramic baking dish with a tight-fitting lid or a Dutch oven.

3 Add the *vi ranci* to the pan. Deglaze over medium heat, stirring to scrape up any browned bits. Let cook until the liquid is reduced by about one-third, about 5 minutes. Add the tomato purée, onion, garlic, parsley, and pimentón. Sauté for about 30 seconds, then pour over the chicken pieces, and stir to coat the pieces in the sauce. Add ½ cup (4 fl oz/125 ml) water, cover, and cook over low heat, stirring occasionally, until the chicken is tender, about 40 minutes.

4 Meanwhile, in a frying pan over medium heat, warm the remaining 1 tablespoon olive oil. Add the shrimp and sauté just until opaque, about 2 minutes. After the chicken cooks for 35 minutes, add the shrimp and pine nuts.

5 Using a mortar and pestle, grind together the liver and almonds. Add the liver mixture to the chicken and shrimp and mix thoroughly. Cook for 5 minutes longer to allow the flavors to mingle, then remove from the heat. Let cool slightly before serving.

Serve with a juicy Spanish rosé with hints of raspberry.

1 cup (5 oz/155 g) all-purpose (plain) flour

Salt and freshly ground pepper

1 chicken, 2–2½ lb (1–1.25 kg), cut into 4-inch (10-cm) pieces (about 12 pieces)

3 tablespoons olive oil

½ cup (4 fl oz/125 ml) *vi ranci,* sweet sherry, or vermouth

1 cup (8 fl oz/250 ml) tomato purée

½ yellow onion, finely chopped

2 or 3 cloves garlic, minced

2 tablespoons finely chopped fresh flat-leaf (Italian) parsley

1 teaspoon pimentón or sweet paprika

16 medium shrimp (prawns) in the shell, about 1 lb (500 g) total weight

1 tablespoon pine nuts

1 chicken liver, trimmed

⅓ cup (2 oz/60 g) blanched almonds

Makes 4 servings

Mar i Muntanya

If there is one Catalan specialty that is liable to surprise even sophisticated diners, it is *mar i muntanya,* literally "sea and mountain." Even the classic paella, with its combination of shellfish and chicken, is a *mar i muntanya* dish. But in areas like the Empordà and along the Costa Brava, as well as in Majorca and Valencia, the fondness for mixing meat and seafood has given rise to some extraordinary dishes.

Perhaps the most accessible and best-known example of this tradition is *pollastre amb gambes.* But there are few limits to variations on this theme. Cuttlefish are cooked with sausages, squid are stuffed with meat, and suckling pig is baked with grouper. You can even enjoy a terrine of pig's feet with snails at a restaurant near Figueres. Food critic Jaume Fàbrega tells of a dish from the marshlands near Valencia that features eel, chicken, and beans. At the furthest extreme, there is a dish from Empordà called simply *mar i muntanya,* whose ingredient list includes shrimp, mussels, langoustines, sausages, pig's feet, rabbit, chicken, snails, and wild mushrooms.

LLOM AMB PRESSECS

Pork Loin with Peaches

Jordi Alsina, arguably Barcelona's finest charcutier, has his shop and headquarters in the neighborhood of Sants. It seems an unprepossessing place, until you realize the amazing variety of homemade sausages, hams, bacon, and all manner of pork products that cram the tiny space. Jordi, whose family has owned and operated the business since 1883, seems to know more than just about anyone about the range of Catalan sausages, and he makes most of them in the butchery behind the shop. This simple dish of roasted pork loin with fresh peaches is similar to a dish made by Alsina.

1 cup (5 oz/155 g) all-purpose
(plain) flour

Salt and freshly ground pepper

4 boneless pork loin chops, about
1 lb (500 g) total weight and each
about ¾ inch (2 cm) thick

⅓ cup (3 fl oz/80 ml) olive oil,
or as needed

½ cup (4 fl oz/125 ml) Cognac

1 yellow onion, chopped

2 tomatoes, peeled, seeded
(page 187), and chopped

2 cups (16 fl oz/500 ml) chicken
stock, or as needed

¾ cup (6 fl oz/180 ml)
peach nectar

3 peaches, about 1 lb (500 g)
total weight

Makes 4 servings

1 Place the flour in a shallow bowl, season with salt and pepper, and stir to combine. Lightly dredge the pork slices on both sides in the seasoned flour, shaking off any excess.

2 In a heavy-bottomed frying pan over medium heat, warm the ⅓ cup olive oil. Add the pork and sauté, turning once, until golden brown, about 3 minutes on each side. Using a slotted spoon, transfer the pork to a warmed *cassola* or flameproof ceramic baking dish and set aside, away from the heat. Reserve the pan with the remaining oil.

3 In a small saucepan over low heat, warm the Cognac, about 15 seconds. Pour over the pork. Averting your face, use a long kitchen match to ignite the Cognac. When the alcohol has burned off, the flames will die out. (Keep a pan lid ready in case the flames flare up.)

4 In the reserved frying pan, make a *sofregit:* Warm the oil remaining in the pan over medium heat (add a little more olive oil if needed). Add the onion and sauté until softened, about 3 minutes. Add the tomatoes and cook until they have darkened in color, 2–3 minutes. Add the stock and the peach nectar and season to taste with salt and pepper. Raise the heat to high and bring to a boil, then reduce the heat to medium-low and let simmer until the sauce begins to thicken, 2–3 minutes. Pour over the pork loin chops in the *cassola.* Cook over medium heat until the pork is tender, about 30 minutes.

5 Meanwhile, peel the peaches: Bring a saucepan three-fourths full of water to a boil. Cut an X in the blossom end of each peach. Immerse in the boiling water until the skin begins to curl away from the X, about 30 seconds. Using a slotted spoon, transfer to a bowl of ice water to cool, then peel away the skin. Cut each peach in half lengthwise, remove the stone, and slice into wedges.

6 Add the peaches to the *cassola,* spooning a bit of the sauce over them. Cook, adding a little more stock if necessary, until the peaches are soft but not falling apart, about 7 minutes longer.

7 Arrange the pork slices neatly on a shallow serving platter and place the peaches around them. Spoon the sauce over the top and serve.

Serve with a fruity, young red wine from the Penedès.

ESCUDELLA I CARN D'OLLA

Two-Course Mixed Stew of Beans, Meats, and Vegetables

In its prime, perhaps thirty years ago, escudella was one of the most familiar of all Catalan dishes. Reportedly, it was served in some households five or six times a week, with the result that many people became heartily fed up with it, and nowadays the dish is much less common than it deserves to be. Similar to a French pot-au-feu, the escudella is basically a slow-cooked stew of mixed meats, vegetables, and beans that is divided into two courses: the broth, to which rice or pasta is usually added, and the carn d'olla (literally, "meat of the pot"), which is served with a vinaigrette.

1 Soak the dried *mongetes del ganxet* or chickpeas overnight in water to cover.

2 Fill a large stockpot two-thirds full of water and add the beef, lamb, *panceta,* chicken, and ham bone. Bring to a boil over high heat, uncovered, skimming off any foam that rises to the surface. Reduce the heat to low and simmer for 1 hour, skimming regularly.

3 Drain the beans, then add to the stockpot and simmer for 1 hour longer.

4 Peel and chop the carrots, parsnips, and turnips. Chop the celery and the white and pale green parts of the leeks. Cut the potatoes into 3-inch (7.5-cm) pieces. Add the carrots, parsnips, turnips, celery, leeks, potatoes, onion, and cabbage to the stockpot and simmer for 1 hour.

5 Meanwhile, make the meatballs: In a bowl, mix together the pork, veal, minced garlic, egg, and half of the parsley and season with salt and pepper. Form the mixture into 10 small balls and dust generously with the flour. Keep in the refrigerator until ready to use.

6 After the stew has simmered a total of 3 hours, the beans should be thoroughly tender, the vegetables softened, and the liquid reduced by half. Taste the broth; it should have enough flavor to stand on its own as a soup. Season generously with salt and pepper.

7 Reduce the heat to low and place the sausages, and meatballs on top of the other ingredients. Cover the pot and cook until the sausages and meatballs are firm and opaque, about 30 minutes.

8 Meanwhile, mince the remaining parsley leaves. In a small bowl, combine the vinegar, crushed garlic, and minced parsley. Add the olive oil in a thin stream, whisking constantly. Season to taste with salt and pepper. Set the *vinagreta* aside.

9 Remove the pot from the heat and ladle out as much of the broth as possible, pouring it through a sieve into a saucepan. In a small frying pan over medium heat, toast the saffron, about 5 seconds. Transfer the saffron to a mortar and pestle and grind to a powder. Add the saffron and *fideos* to the broth and simmer over low heat until the noodles are soft, about 4 minutes. Ladle into soup bowls for the first course.

10 To serve the second course, slice the sausages and arrange the meat and vegetables on a separate serving platter. Drizzle with some of the *vinagreta* and serve the remaining *vinagreta* on the side.

Serve with a concentrated, powerful Spanish red wine from the Priorat.

1 cup (7 oz/220 g) dried *mongetes del ganxet* or chickpeas (garbanzos)

1-lb (500-g) piece *each* beef rib, stewing lamb, and *panceta*

½ chicken, about 1 lb (500 g)

6-oz (185-g) piece ham bone

2 *each* carrots, parsnips, turnips, celery stalks, and leeks

4 russet potatoes, peeled

1 large yellow onion, chopped

¼ head green cabbage, sliced

6 oz (185 g) *each* ground (minced) pork and veal

3 cloves garlic, 2 minced and 1 crushed

1 large egg

Leaves of 8 sprigs fresh flat-leaf (Italian) parsley

Salt and freshly ground pepper

All-purpose (plain) flour for dusting

2 blood sausages (optional)

½ lb (250 g) raw pork sausages

2 tablespoons red wine vinegar

½ cup (4 fl oz/125 ml) olive oil

Generous pinch of saffron threads

5 oz (155 g) *fideos* or vermicelli

Makes 10–12 servings

ÀNEC AMB PANSES I CASTANYES

Roast Duck with Raisins and Chestnuts

While barely seen in other parts of Spain, duck is increasingly common in Barcelona, thanks to the French influence, where the dish is practically omnipresent along the border of Catalonia. Traditional preparations of duck include braising it with turnips or roasting it with apples. This is not one of those classic dishes, but it is so authentically Catalan in spirit that it might as well be. This recipe is inspired by one from Josep Lladonosa i Giró, one of Catalonia's most famous gastronomes. His book, La Cuina Que Torna, published in 1979, revolutionized the Catalan food scene with many recipes that were then either extinct or rarely seen.

¾ cup (4½ oz/140 g) raisins

½ lb (250 g) fresh chestnuts, blanched and peeled (page 185), or vacuum-packed chestnuts

Salt and freshly ground pepper

1 duck, about 3 lb (1.5 kg)

Generous pinch of freshly grated nutmeg

2 small yellow onions, coarsely chopped

1 tablespoon all-purpose (plain) flour

1 cup (8 fl oz/250 ml) dry white wine

1 cup (8 fl oz/250 ml) *moscatel* or other sweet wine

⅓ cup (2 oz/60 g) pine nuts

Makes 4 servings

1 In a bowl, soak the raisins in cold water to cover until they have plumped up slightly, about 1 hour. Drain and set aside.

2 If using fresh chestnuts, bring a large saucepan three-fourths full of water to a boil. Salt the water, add the chestnuts, and cook until tender but still whole and not mushy, about 10 minutes. Drain and set aside.

3 Preheat the oven to 350°F (180°C). Remove any giblets from the cavity of the duck and reserve for another use or discard. Rinse the duck inside and out and pat dry. Holding the blade of a sharp knife almost parallel to the skin, push the tip through the skin to make small slits all over the breast and thighs. Do not penetrate the flesh. This will help release some of the fat when the duck is roasting. Season well inside and out with salt and pepper and the nutmeg. Place in a roasting pan breast side up and roast until the duck is beginning to brown on top, about 45 minutes.

4 Surround the duck with the onions and roast for 15 minutes longer. Add the chestnuts, sprinkle them evenly with the flour, and stir to combine with the onions. Pour the white wine and *moscatel* over the duck and roast for 15 minutes longer.

5 Using a wooden spoon or spatula to lift the bird, tip any cooking juices from the cavity into the onion and chestnut mixture and then transfer the duck to a platter. Add the raisins and pine nuts to the pan, season to taste with salt and pepper, and stir well, distributing the mixture evenly over the bottom of the pan. Return the duck to the pan and roast until the skin is golden brown and crisp, 10–20 minutes longer.

6 Transfer the duck to a serving platter and, using a slotted spoon, arrange the chestnuts, raisins, pine nuts, and onions around the duck. Alternatively, transfer the duck to a carving board and cut into serving pieces with a large, sharp knife or heavy-duty kitchen scissors. Arrange on a serving dish, skin side up, with the chestnuts, raisins, pine nuts, and onions.

7 To serve, skim off as much fat as possible from the pan juices, then drizzle over the duck and pass the rest at the table.

Serve with a complex, powerful red wine such as an oak-aged red from the Priorat.

CIVET DE PORC

Pork Stew with Picada

In 1975, Josep Maria Boix opened a restaurant in the mountains of the Cerdanya. Almost thirty years later, it has become one of the best-loved restaurants in Catalonia—so much so that Josep Maria opened a branch in Barcelona, called Boix de Cerdanya. The restaurant serves as an urban showcase for the earthy and powerful cuisine of the Pyrenees—of which civet de senglar, *a delicious dish of wild boar simmered in red wine, is one of the high points. This is a version of that traditional recipe that works well for pork. The* picada, *a rich, nutty paste featuring dark chocolate, is reminiscent of Mexican mole.*

1 Cut the pork into 2-inch (5-cm) cubes. In a large glass or nonreactive bowl, combine the pork, onion, carrots, leek, tomatoes, garlic, lemon, peppercorns, thyme, and bay leaves. Add the wine, cover, and marinate in the refrigerator, stirring once, for at least 24 hours or up to 2 days.

2 Transfer the pork cubes to a colander to drain. Reserve the remaining marinade ingredients in the bowl. Dry the pork with a clean kitchen towel.

3 In a Dutch oven or other heavy-bottomed pot with a lid over medium heat, melt the butter with the olive oil. Working in batches, add the pork and cook, turning as needed, until lightly browned on all sides, about 8 minutes. Using a slotted spoon, transfer the pork to a plate. Strain the reserved marinade. Set aside the liquid and discard the lemon half. Raise the heat under the pot to medium-high, add the vegetables and herbs from the marinade, and sauté them in the same oil used for the pork until the onion is softened and almost all the liquid has evaporated, about 5 minutes. Remove from the heat.

4 Bring the strained marinade liquid to a boil in a small saucepan over high heat and cook until reduced by half, about 15 minutes.

5 Return the pork to the pot holding the vegetables. Add the reduced marinade and enough of the stock to cover the meat (you may not need all of the stock; be sure to reserve at least ½ cup/4 fl oz/125 ml). Place over low heat and simmer, uncovered, until the pork is fork-tender, about 1 hour.

6 Remove from the heat and, using the slotted spoon, transfer the pork to a bowl. Discard the bay leaves, thyme sprig, and peppercorns. Push the rest of the sauce through a fine-mesh sieve. Alternatively, process briefly in a food processor. Return both the sauce and pork to the pot, season with salt, stir well, cover, and continue to simmer gently over low heat, adding a little more stock if the mixture seems dry, until the sauce is thick, 10–15 minutes.

7 To make the *picada,* cut off the crust from the bread slice. In a small frying pan over medium-high heat, fry the bread in the olive oil until crisp, about 2 minutes. Remove from the heat. Using a mortar and pestle, grind together the bread, nuts, chocolate, and parsley until a dark, rich-smelling, crumbly paste forms. Stir the *picada* into the sauce and let it simmer gently for 5–10 minutes, being careful not to let it burn.

8 Transfer the stew to a warmed serving platter or bowl and serve.

Serve with a dense, smooth red wine with aromas of forest fruit such as Ribera del Duero.

2 lb (1 kg) boneless fresh leg of pork or pork shoulder butt

1 large yellow onion, thinly sliced

2 carrots, peeled and chopped

1 leek, white and pale green parts, chopped

2 ripe tomatoes, chopped

6 cloves garlic, peeled and crushed

½ lemon

8 black peppercorns

1 fresh thyme sprig

2 bay leaves

1 bottle (24 fl oz/750 ml) red wine

1 tablespoon unsalted butter

¼ cup (2 fl oz/60 ml) olive oil

3 cups (24 fl oz/750 ml) beef stock, or as needed

Salt

1 small slice coarse country bread

1 tablespoon olive oil

6 blanched almonds; 4 hazelnuts (filberts), skinned (page 173); 4 walnuts; and 1 tablespoon pine nuts

1 oz (30 g) bittersweet chocolate

Handful of fresh flat-leaf (Italian) parsley leaves

Makes 4 servings

COSTELLES DE XAI A LA LLOSA AMB OLI D'HERBES

Stone-Cooked Lamb Chops with Herb Oil

A la llosa, *literally "on the stone," refers to a technique for cooking meat on a flat stone placed over an open fire. The meat is briefly seared on a garlic-rubbed slab of slate, yielding tender and juicy results with a smoky aroma from the hot stone. Common in farmhouses and rural kitchens, this technique is now popping up on restaurant menus in Barcelona. You can re-create it with a cast-iron griddle or heavy frying pan, or better still, invest in a cooking stone like the Italian one made by Olare that fits into a metal frame with handles, enabling you to cook Pyrenean style directly at the table.*

FOR THE HERB OIL
2 fresh sage leaves

1 bay leaf, crumbled

Leaves from 4 fresh flat-leaf (Italian) parsley sprigs

Leaves from 3 fresh mint sprigs

Leaves from 3 fresh basil sprigs

Leaves from 1 fresh marjoram sprig

Leaves from 1 fresh oregano sprig

Leaves from 2 arugula (rocket) sprigs

1 tablespoon chopped fresh chives

1 clove garlic, peeled

1 cup (8 fl oz/250 ml) extra-virgin olive oil

Salt and freshly ground pepper

1 clove garlic, halved

12 thin-cut lamb chops each about 3 oz (90 g) and ½ inch (12 mm) thick

Salt and freshly ground pepper

Lemon wedges for serving

Makes 6 servings

1 To make the herb oil, using a large mortar and pestle, grind together the sage, bay leaf, parsley, mint, basil, marjoram, oregano, arugula, chives, and garlic until a thick paste forms. Add the olive oil in a thin stream, continuing to mash the herbs, to make a bright green, fragrant sauce. Season to taste with salt and pepper.

2 Rub a griddle, frying pan, or cooking stone (see Note) with the cut sides of the garlic halves. Heat the pan over high heat until sizzling hot. Season the lamb chops with salt and pepper. Working in batches, sear the chops briefly on both sides until just cooked through, about 2 minutes on each side. Be careful not to overcook the lamb, as it dries out easily.

3 Drizzle the chops with the herb oil and serve at once with the lemon wedges on the side.

Serve with a well-rounded, aromatic red wine from the Ribera del Duero.

ORADA A LA SAL

Whole Fish Baked in Salt

Packing a whole fish in rock salt is one of the best ways to cook it. The salt keeps the flesh moist and seems to lock in the flavor of the fish, while the skin acts as a barrier to lock out the intense saltiness. The whole fish emerging from its salty tomb is a spectacle in itself, but the real beauty of this dish is its total simplicity. You need serve nothing more alongside than a green vegetable—perhaps steamed green beans with butter—and baby new potatoes. If you like, pass a bowl of freshly made allioli *(page 105) for guests to help themselves.*

1 Preheat the oven to 475°F (245°C). Butter a baking dish large enough to hold the fish comfortably.

2 Place the fish in the prepared dish and cover evenly and completely with the rock salt. Bake until the salt has formed a hard crust, about 45 minutes.

3 Using a large stainless-steel spoon, remove as much of the salt as possible. Skin and fillet the fish carefully, and transfer the fillets to individual plates.

4 Season with a generous grinding of pepper and serve with the lemon wedges.

Serve with a fragrant, fruity white Albariño from Galicia or a Penedès white.

Unsalted butter for greasing

1 whole *dorada* (gilthead bream), red snapper, or other firm-fleshed fish, about 3 lb (1.5 kg), cleaned and scaled by the fishmonger

4 lb (2 kg) rock salt

Freshly ground pepper

1 lemon, cut into wedges

Makes 4 servings

Salt

Salt plays an important role in the culinary and economic history of the Catalan lands. The coastal salt flats of Santa Pola and Torrevieja, and also those on the island of Ibiza, have been a vital source of income at least since the days of the Phoenicians, who established the salt trade across the Mediterranean basin. The technique of encasing food, particularly seafood, in salt and then baking it, originated in the salt-producing regions of the Alicante. As one of the most basic forms of food preservation, salt is still used in the production of Catalan hams and *embotits* (sausages) and in salt cod, or *bacallà*. Although it originates in Iceland and the Faroe Islands, *bacallà* is a perfect example of the preservative qualities of salt.

Salt is widely used throughout Spanish cuisine, and non-Spaniards often remark on the amount of salt used in the local cooking. Tapas, which are designed to accompany beer and wine, are often highly salted as an incentive to drink more. In fact, the local appetite for salty foods seems to be natural in a hot climate, where the body needs more of this vital substance.

FIDEUÀ

Vegetable and Seafood Noodles

According to legend, in the harbor town of Gandía, a fisherman was about to make a paella with the fish and shellfish he had just caught. Discovering he had no rice, he used pasta instead—and fideuà *was born. It is now one of the most popular dishes in the Catalan repertoire, and most restaurants along the old port of Barcelona include it on the menu. The name comes from* fideo *(*fideu *in Catalan), the generic term for pasta common all over Spain. In this case, it refers to a short, thin macaroni. As with paella, the success of* fideuà *depends largely on the quality of the stock. Serve with crusty country bread.*

½ lb (250 g) medium shrimp (prawns) in the shell

1½ lb (750 g) fish heads and bones

12 large mussels, about 1 lb (500 g) total weight

12 large clams, about 1 lb (500 g) total weight

4 ripe tomatoes, about 1 lb (500 g) total weight, cored

Sea salt

½ teaspoon saffron threads

½ cup (4 fl oz/125 ml) olive oil

½ lb (250 g) grouper or other firm-fleshed fish fillets, cut into 1-inch (2.5-cm) cubes

1 large red bell pepper (capsicum), seeded and cut into ½-inch (12-mm) dice

½ lb (250 g) *fideos* or other short, thin macaroni

4 cloves garlic, minced

Handful of fresh flat-leaf (Italian) parsley leaves, minced

Makes 4–6 servings

1 In a stockpot over high heat, bring 5 cups (40 fl oz/ 1.25 l) water to a boil. Meanwhile, peel the shrimp and add the heads and shells to the water; set the peeled shrimp aside. Add the fish heads and bones and return to a boil, skimming off any foam. Reduce the heat to medium-low and simmer gently, uncovered, until the liquid has reduced by one-third, about 30 minutes. Strain the stock through a colander or sieve lined with cheesecloth (muslin) placed over a bowl. Return the strained stock to the stockpot.

2 Scrub the mussels and clams with a stiff brush. Debeard the mussels by scraping off the tuft of fibers with a knife. Pour water to a depth of 1 inch (2.5 cm) into a wide saucepan over medium-high heat. Add the mussels, discarding any that do not close to the touch, cover, and cook, shaking the pan occasionally, until they open, about 5 minutes. Using a slotted spoon, remove the mussels and set aside, discarding any that failed to open. Reserve the pan and water.

3 Using the same pan and water, cook the clams in the same way and set aside. Strain the cooking water through a colander or sieve lined with cheesecloth and add to the stockpot.

4 Halve the tomatoes, grate the flesh on the large holes of a grater-shredder into a bowl, and discard the skins. Set aside. Using a mortar and pestle, grind 1 teaspoon salt with the saffron until a deep yellow powder forms. Set aside.

5 In a 16-inch (40-cm) paella pan or wide, heavy frying pan over medium heat, warm the olive oil. Add the peeled shrimp and cook, turning in the hot oil, until opaque throughout, about 1 minute. Transfer to a bowl with the slotted spoon. Cook the fish cubes in the same way until opaque, about 2 minutes. Transfer with the slotted spoon to the bowl with the shrimp. Add the bell pepper and sauté until just soft, about 2 minutes, then transfer with the slotted spoon to the bowl with the shrimp and fish.

6 Add the macaroni, garlic, and parsley to the pan and fry in the hot oil until fragrant and the macaroni is coated in oil, about 30 seconds. Add the tomato pulp, mixing well, and sauté for 30 seconds longer. Pour in 4 cups (32 fl oz/1 l) of the fish stock and add the shrimp, fish, bell pepper, and saffron mixture, stirring to distribute the ingredients evenly. Reduce the heat to low and simmer gently, without stirring, until almost all of the stock is absorbed by the macaroni, about 20 minutes. After the macaroni has been cooking for about 10 minutes, arrange the mussels and clams (in their shells) on the surface.

7 Turn off the heat and cover the pan with a clean kitchen towel. Let rest for about 10 minutes to allow the flavors to mingle thoroughly and the macaroni to absorb any remaining juices. Serve warm, not hot.

Serve with a slightly sparkling, crisp white wine.

POSTRES

Whether homemade or available at the neighborhood *pastisseries*,

the sweet flavors of Barcelona offer something for everyone.

Spanish cuisine is not well known for desserts, but the more closely you look, the more variety and quality you will see. French-influenced pastries come together with traditional sweets of the Catalan kitchen to create a surprisingly wide dessert repertoire, from simple classics like *mel i mató* (fresh cheese with honey) to more complex preparations. It is quite acceptable in Barcelona to buy cakes, tarts, and the like from the *pastisseria,* although traditional desserts such as *crema catalana* and *flam* are almost always homemade. Catalans appreciate locally harvested fruit, and a selection of them makes an authentically Mediterranean finish to a meal.

MEL I MATÓ AMB FIGUES

Fresh Cheese and Honey with Figs

Mató is a fresh cheese no more than a day or two old. Pearly white, cool, and creamy, with the taste of fresh milk, it is a cheese that is only just barely a cheese. Formerly made from goat's or sheep's milk, but now often from cow's, the best examples come from Montserrat, the mountain range outside Barcelona, and from the village of Fonteta, near Girona. The most most widely available equivalent is probably ricotta, although any fresh curd cheese will work. Sprinkled with a little sugar, mató is a favorite breakfast food throughout Catalonia.

1 If using *mató,* cut the cheese into slices 1 inch (2.5 cm) thick and arrange on individual plates. Alternatively, if the cheese is not solid enough to slice, divide it evenly and spoon it onto each plate.

2 Using a small, sharp knife, remove the woody stems from the figs. Cut each fig into quarters lengthwise and arrange them, flesh side up, next to the cheese on each plate.

3 Drizzle the honey evenly over the cheese and figs and serve at once.

Serve with a golden, silky *moscatel* from Alicante.

1 lb (500 g) *mató* or whole-milk ricotta cheese

4–6 ripe figs, about 6 oz (185 g) total weight

½ cup (6 oz/185 g) light, aromatic honey such as orange blossom

Makes 4 servings

Honey

The ancient Romans believed that the best honeys in the Mediterranean came from Greece. But the second-best honeys, they insisted, were from the Balearic Islands. Majorca and Ibiza still produce exquisite honey on a domestic scale, but the focus of the industry has shifted to other parts of Spain. Catalonia now claims over sixty-five thousand beehives, and areas like Port de Beseit in the south of the region and Pla de Bages in the north are known for their fragrant artisan honeys.

The most common type of honey in Catalonia is *milflores* (thousand flowers), followed by honeys derived from thyme, rosemary, or heather. But the most highly valued honey in Spain is *azahar,* or orange blossom, hailing from the extensive orange plantations outside Valencia.

Honey is used in unique ways in Catalan cooking; it turns up in *alberginies dolces,* eggplant (aubergine) fritters drizzled with honey, and is paired with almonds to make the Christmas nougat *turrón.* Perhaps the oddest use is in *bacallà amb mel,* salt cod with honey, a Catalan ode to medieval cuisine.

CREMA CATALANA

Catalan Burnt Cream

Crema catalana is traditionally made for the feast of Saint Joseph on March 16, but it is also an everyday delicacy enjoyed throughout the region. You'd be hard pressed to find a Barcelona restaurant menu that doesn't feature crema catalana. The bad news, given such popularity, is that it is a little tricky to make. The consistency of the custard must be neither jellylike nor excessively liquid, but just solid enough to be eaten in deliciously creamy spoonfuls. Traditionally, a spiral iron is heated until extremely hot, then used to create the brittle sugar crust. A kitchen torch or broiler can be substituted with excellent results.

8 large egg yolks

¾ cup (6 oz/185 g) sugar

4½ tablespoons (1 oz/30 g) cornstarch (cornflour)

4 cups (32 fl oz/1 l) whole milk

Grated zest of ½ lemon

3-inch (7.5-cm) piece cinnamon stick

Makes 6 servings

1 In a bowl, using a balloon whisk, beat together the egg yolks and ½ cup (4 oz/125 g) of the sugar until pale and creamy, about 6 minutes.

2 In a large bowl, dissolve the cornstarch in ¼ cup (2 fl oz/60 ml) of the milk. In a heavy-bottomed saucepan over low heat, combine the remaining 3¾ cups (30 fl oz/940 ml) milk, the lemon zest, and the cinnamon stick and heat until bubbles form along the edges of the pan, about 10 minutes.

3 Whisk the egg yolk mixture into the cornstarch mixture until well blended. Add a little of the hot milk, whisking constantly to prevent the yolks from curdling. Add the remaining milk little by little while continuing to whisk.

4 Strain the mixture through a fine-mesh sieve back into the saucepan used for heating the milk. Heat slowly over very low heat, stirring constantly, until the mixture thickens into a custard, about 15 minutes. Do not let it boil or the mixture will curdle.

5 Pour the custard into six 1-cup (8–fl oz/250-ml) shallow custard dishes or ramekins or into a 2-qt (2-l) shallow gratin dish and let cool to room temperature. Cover with plastic wrap and refrigerate until well chilled, at least 2 hours or up to 12 hours.

6 Make the sugar crust no more than 30 minutes before serving, or the topping will be soggy instead of crisp. Dust the surface of the cold custard evenly with the remaining ¼ cup (2 oz/60 g) sugar, dividing it evenly if using individual dishes.

7 Using a kitchen torch, and holding it 2–3 inches (5–7.5 cm) from the surface, caramelize the sugar by constantly moving the flame over the top until the sugar bubbles. Alternatively, preheat the broiler (grill). Place the ramekins or gratin dish on a baking sheet and place under the broiler 3 inches (7.5 cm) from the heat source. Broil (grill) until the top is caramelized, about 2 minutes. The burnt sugar should form a thin sheet of golden brown caramel.

Serve with an intense, richly flavored *moscatel*.

POSTRE DEL MÚSIC
Musician's Dessert

The name of this dish alludes to the musicians of the cobal, the wind bands that played at the banquets of the medieval era. Els músics were commonly served with a bowl of fruit and nuts and a flagon of wine to keep up their strength. Nowadays "the musician's dessert" is brought out at the end of a meal or in the afternoon or early evening, when a few people might be gathered around the table for a chat and suddenly feel a little hungry. A glass or two of sweet wine is considered a mandatory accompaniment for this dessert.

1 In a small frying pan over medium-high heat, toast the hazelnuts until the skins begin to darken and visibly loosen, about 3 minutes. Remove from the heat and rub off the skins with a clean, dry kitchen towel. Set aside to cool.

2 In the same pan over medium-high heat, toast the blanched almonds until golden brown, about 1 minute. Pour onto a plate to cool. In the same pan over medium-high heat, toast the walnuts until lightly colored, about 1 minute. Pour onto a plate to cool.

3 Combine the cooled nuts and dried fruits in a serving dish, or arrange decoratively on individual plates before serving.

Serve with a moscatel, Malvasia, or other dessert wine.

½ cup (2½ oz/75 g) hazelnuts (filberts)

½ cup (2½ oz/75 g) blanched almonds

½ cup (2 oz/60 g) walnuts

2 cups (12 oz/375 g) mixed dried fruits such as raisins, dates, prunes, figs, and apricots

Makes 6 servings

Dessert Wines

To satisfy their sweet tooth, Catalans like nothing better than a glass of sweet wine with dessert, in the afternoon with cookies or cake, or even as a midday *aperitiu* (aperitif). The range of sweet wines in Catalonia is broad and complex, although none is made in large quantities. Most famous and characteristic are the *rancis* of Tarragona, a traditional style of highly alcoholic wine that is aged for a minimum of four years. *Vi ranci* is widely used in Catalan cooking.

The *vins dolços,* or sweet wines, of the Empordá, made with the Garnatxa grape, are also old-fashioned wines, relatively strong in alcohol and usually aged for two years or more in oak.

Malvasia de Sitges is one of the rarest wines in Spain, made in tiny quantities in the town of Sitges near Barcelona. It has a velvety richness nicely balanced with acidity that is reminiscent of orange marmalade. *Ratafia,* a specialty of Lleida and the surrounding *comarques* (counties), is an unusual treat: a sweet infusion of walnuts and spices, taken as an aperitif or postprandial tipple.

MONA DE XOCOLATA

Chocolate Truffle Cake

Come Easter time, a category of artful cakes starts appearing in the windows of grand Barcelona pastisseries like Escribà and Fargas. From simple chocolate cakes to vast sculptures made entirely of chocolate, mona de Pasqua, Catalonia's Easter cake par excellence, takes a wide variety of forms. Nearly all modern mones are coated in some form of chocolate, and the grandest mones of all—the ones that hit the headlines in the local press—are positive works of art. This recipe, from Chocovic, Catalonia's dynamic chocolate company, falls halfway between an old-fashioned and a modern mona.

FOR THE CHOCOLATE CREAM

1½ cups (12 fl oz/375 ml) heavy (double) cream

¼ cup (2 oz/60 g) sugar

5 oz (155 g) bittersweet chocolate, grated

FOR THE CAKE

1¼ cups (10 oz/315 g) unsalted butter, at room temperature

6 large eggs, at room temperature

1¼ cups (10 oz/315 g) sugar

2 cups (10 oz/315 g) all-purpose (plain) flour

FOR THE SYRUP

½ cup (4 oz/125 g) sugar

1 cup (8 fl oz/250 ml) water

7 oz (220 g) bittersweet chocolate, broken into small pieces

Chocolate eggs (optional)

Makes 10–12 servings

1 To make the chocolate cream, in a small saucepan over low heat, bring the cream to a gentle simmer. Add the sugar and stir until dissolved. Add the grated chocolate and stir until the chocolate is melted. Let cool, then cover and refrigerate for 24 hours.

2 To make the sponge cake, preheat the oven to 375°F (190°C). Butter a 10-inch (25-cm) cake pan. Dust with flour and tap out the excess.

3 In a bowl, cream the butter with a wooden spoon until pale and fluffy. In a separate bowl, using a handheld mixer or balloon whisk, beat together the eggs and sugar until the mixture is pale and triples in volume. Add the butter a little at a time, beating constantly, until thoroughly combined. Sift the flour into the butter mixture and mix well.

4 Pour the batter into the prepared pan. Bake the cake until golden brown on top and a skewer inserted into the center comes out clean, about 50 minutes. Transfer to a wire rack to cool.

5 To make the syrup, in a small saucepan, combine the sugar and water. Bring to a boil over medium heat and cook until a syrupy consistency forms, about 4 minutes. Do not let it turn golden. Remove from the heat and set aside to cool.

6 Place the chocolate pieces in the top pan of a double boiler or in a stainless-steel bowl. Set the pan or bowl over (not touching) barely simmering water in a saucepan. Heat until the chocolate melts, stirring occasionally. Do not allow any steam to come into contact with the chocolate.

7 Pour the chocolate onto a cool, smooth surface (ideally a marble or polished stone surface), allowing it to spread into a wafer-thin layer. Let cool completely. With a sharp, heavy knife, shave away the chocolate from the surface, forming delicate curls.

8 To assemble the cake, remove the chocolate cream from the refrigerator and beat with a handheld mixer or balloon whisk until it is thick enough to spread with a knife. Using a large, serrated knife, cut the sponge cake horizontally into 2 equal layers. Place the bottom half of the cake, cut side up, on a serving plate. Brush half of the syrup over the cut side, then spread with about half of the chocolate cream, creating a thick coating. Carefully place the top half of the cake, cut side up, over the chocolate cream, and top it with the remaining syrup and then the remaining chocolate cream. Decorate the cake with the chocolate curls and with the chocolate eggs, if using.

Serve with a rich, plummy Port or other fortified dessert wine from the Penedès.

FLAÓ EIVISSENC

Ibiza Goat Cheese Tart with Mint

The culture on the island of Ibiza has much in common with Catalan culture; in fact, it is considered part of the països catalans, *or Catalan lands. On one small farm, an elderly peasant lady named Maria kept a small herd of goats and made fresh cheese, which formed the basis of her superb* flaó. *Maria insisted on two ingredients in her* flaó *that made it into something special: a spoonful of aniseeds in the pastry dough and a sprinkling of fresh mint in the filling. The mint cuts the richness of the tart with a hint of freshness. You can also use fresh cow's cheese instead, which has a milder flavor.*

1 To make the dough, sift the flour into a bowl. Make a well in the center, and add the aniseeds, liqueur, and oil. Using your fingertips, lightly mix the flour with the other ingredients until the mixture resembles coarse bread crumbs. Add 3 tablespoons of the water and continue to mix until the mixture comes together into a smooth, elastic dough, adding the remaining tablespoon of water if needed.

2 Butter a 9-inch (23-cm) tart pan with a removable bottom. On a lightly floured work surface, roll out the dough into an 11-inch (28-cm) round about ¼ inch (6 mm) thick. Transfer the round to the prepared tart pan, pressing it smoothly against the bottom and sides. Trim the edges even with the pan rim. Set the pastry-lined pan aside.

3 Preheat the oven to 350°F (180°C). To make the filling, in a bowl, lightly mash the cheese with a fork. Add the eggs, granulated sugar, and lemon zest. Tear the mint leaves into very small pieces and add to the bowl. Mix well and pour into the pastry shell.

4 Bake the tart until the top is pale gold, about 30 minutes. Transfer the tart to a wire rack and let cool completely. The filling may puff up slightly but will settle as it begins to cool.

5 Remove the pan sides and carefully slide the tart onto a plate. Using a fine-mesh sieve or sifter, dust the top of the tart with confectioners' sugar, if using. Cut into wedges to serve.

Serve with a mahogany-colored dessert wine made from the Pedro Ximénez grape.

FOR THE DOUGH

1¾ cups (9 oz/280 g) all-purpose (plain) flour

1 teaspoon aniseeds

¼ cup (2 fl oz/60 ml) anise liqueur such as *anis seco*, Pernod, or pastis

¼ cup (2 fl oz/60 ml) canola or mild vegetable oil

4 tablespoons (2 fl oz/60 ml) water

Unsalted butter for greasing

FOR THE FILLING

1 lb (500 g) *mató* (page 60) or whole-milk ricotta cheese

4 large eggs, beaten

1 cup (8 oz/250 g) granulated sugar

Grated zest of 1 lemon

4 fresh mint leaves

Confectioners' (icing) sugar for dusting (optional)

Makes one 9-inch (23-cm) tart, or 6 servings

PA DE PESSIC AMB AVELLANES I REGALESSIA

Hazelnut Cake with Licorice

Espai Sucre is a restaurant unlike any other in Barcelona, in Catalonia, or perhaps in the world: it serves only desserts. And what desserts! Chef Jordi Butrón trained with Ferran Adrià, the famed chef of the restaurant El Bulli in Roses, and has inherited something of the master's original take on ingredients, not to mention the scientific precision with which he works on his sweet creations. The following is Butrón's version of the classic Catalan sponge cake, or pa de pessic, *featuring toasted hazelnuts and a spoonful of ground licorice, which gives the cake a delicious and aromatic kick.*

1½ cups (7½ oz/235 g) hazelnuts (filberts)

4 large eggs, at room temperature

1 cup (8 oz/250 g) granulated sugar

1 cup (8 oz/250 g) unsalted butter, at room temperature

1 cup (5 oz/155 g) all-purpose (plain) flour

2 teaspoons ground licorice (see Note)

Confectioners' (icing) sugar for dusting (optional)

Makes 6 servings

1 Preheat the oven to 375°F (190°C). Butter a 10-inch (25-cm) cake pan. Dust with flour and tap out the excess.

2 In a small frying pan over medium-high heat, toast the hazelnuts until the skins begin to darken and visibly loosen, about 3 minutes. Remove from the heat and rub off the skins with a clean, dry kitchen towel. Put half of the hazelnuts into a food processor and process just until it becomes a fine powder, being careful not to overprocess. Wrap the remaining half of the hazelnuts in a clean, dry kitchen towel and gently break into pieces with a mallet.

3 In a bowl, using a whisk, beat together the eggs and granulated sugar until the mixture becomes a pale, creamy mousse and has tripled in volume, about 5 minutes. Add the butter little by little while continuing to whisk. Then add the flour, ground hazelnuts, hazelnut pieces, and licorice and mix well.

4 Pour the batter into the prepared pan. Bake until a skewer inserted into the center comes out clean, about 50 minutes. Let cool slightly on a wire rack. Run a table knife around the inside edge of the pan to loosen the cake, then invert the cake onto a serving plate. Using a fine-mesh sieve or sifter, dust the top of the cake with confectioners' sugar, if using. Serve the cake warm or at room temperature.

Serve with a nutty, rich, full-bodied aged sherry.

Note: Ground licorice powder can be found in some specialty and natural-food stores, or it can be made by grinding dried licorice root in a spice grinder or food processor.

GRANISSAT DE CAVA

"Liquid" Granita of Sparkling Wine

Barcelona is one of the most northerly of Spain's major cities, yet it has the climate of the southern Mediterranean. On some days in midsummer, the temperature soars to 105°F (40°C) and higher, and the humidity can make the city feel sticky and uncomfortable. Barcelonans who can afford it disappear to the mountains for the entire month of August. Those who remain do their best to take life easy, with strolls along the old harbor in the evening, an afternoon dip in the sea at one of the city beaches, and a cooling granissat any time of the day.

1 Pour the wine into a shallow metal pan that will fit in the freezer. Freeze it, uncovered, until almost solid, about 3 hours.

2 Remove the pan from the freezer and break up the ice with a fork, scraping it from the sides of the pan. Add the sugar and the lemon zest and juice and mix thoroughly with a fork. If you prefer a sweeter taste, add more sugar. Return to the freezer for 1 hour.

3 Tear the mint leaves into very small pieces, add to the ice mixture, and mix again with a fork, breaking up the ice mixture into small crystals. Spoon into tall glasses and let stand for about 10 minutes to melt slightly. By the time you serve the granita, it should be just liquid enough to drink through a straw.

1 bottle (24 fl oz/750 ml) good-quality dry *cava* or other brut sparkling wine

2 tablespoons sugar, or more as needed

Minced zest and juice of 1 lemon

4–6 fresh mint leaves

Makes 4–6 servings

Cava

Cava is Spain's celebration wine, popular at Christmas and New Year celebrations when it is drunk with the *turróns* and other nougats and sweets at the end of a festive banquet. Until recently *cava* had a reputation as a "poor man's fizz" and was usually thin and acidic. Since the 1990s, however, it has improved remarkably. It is now one of the better sparkling wines on the international market and offers superb value for the money.

The best-known *cava* producers are found in Catalonia, where almost eleven million cases are made annually. It is made according to the French *methode champenoise,* using local white grape varieties, Macabeo, Parellada, and Xarel.lo, plus Chardonnay from the New World. Depending on the degree of sweetness, *cava* may be described on the bottle as *extra-brut, brut, brut nature, extra seco, seco, semi-seco,* or *dulce.* Among the best-known producers of *cava* are Juvé i Camps, Codorníu, Freixenet, Segura Viudas.

An annual Festa del *Cava* is held in October in the town of Sant Sadurní d'Anoia, the capital of *cava* production.

FLAM

Crème Caramel

Flam (or flan in Spanish) is a dish whose popularity in Spain cuts across all borders. You can hardly avoid coming across it at some point during a stay in Barcelona, especially if you happen to visit one of the hundreds of bars and restaurants offering a reasonably priced menú del día. The wobbly milk-and-egg custard with a crown of caramel is one of the most memorable finishes to a meal. It is normally prepared in individual metal pots known as flaneras, specially made for the purpose. Since they can be difficult to find outside Spain, individual-sized ramekins or small custard cups may be substituted.

**3 tablespoons sugar, plus
1 cup (8 oz/250 g)**

2 tablespoons water

**2½ cups (20 fl oz/625 ml)
whole milk**

**1 vanilla bean, split lengthwise,
or a few drops of vanilla
extract (essence)**

**2 large whole eggs plus
6 egg yolks**

Makes 6 servings

1 In a small saucepan, combine the 3 tablespoons sugar and the water. Bring to a boil over medium heat and boil, without stirring, until the mixture becomes a golden brown syrup, about 4 minutes.

2 Pour an equal amount of the caramel syrup into each of six ½-cup (4-fl oz/125-ml) *flaneras*, ramekins, or custard cups, tipping and rotating the molds until the sides are coated about halfway up.

3 Pour the milk into a saucepan, add the vanilla bean, and place over low heat until small bubbles appear along the edge of the pan, about 7 minutes. Do not allow the milk to boil.

4 Preheat the oven to 300°F (150°C). In a bowl, using a balloon whisk, beat together the eggs, egg yolks, and the 1 cup sugar until a pale, creamy mousse forms. Add a little of the hot milk, whisking constantly to prevent the yolks from curdling. Add the remaining milk little by little while continuing to whisk. Strain the custard through a fine-mesh sieve into the prepared molds, dividing it evenly.

5 Place the filled molds in a large baking dish and carefully add boiling water to reach halfway up the sides of the molds.

6 Bake the custards until they are set but the centers still jiggle just slightly, 50–60 minutes. Touch the surface of the custard lightly with the point of a knife; it should come away cleanly when set. Remove the baking dish from the oven, and lift the molds out of the water. Let cool to room temperature, then cover and refrigerate until well chilled, at least 2 hours or up to 6 hours.

7 To serve, run a sharp, thin knife blade around the inside of each mold, and turn out the custards onto individual plates.

Serve with a light, honeyed dessert wine from Navarre.

GLOSSARY

ALLIOLI This pale, pungent sauce gets its heady flavor from raw garlic and its thickness from olive oil. Much loved in Spain, it is often served as a dip or sauce for fish, shellfish, meats, vegetables, or rice dishes. It is traditionally prepared with a mortar and pestle and may include honey, nuts, herbs, or puréed fruit such as quince, apple, or pear.

ANCHOVIES See page 49.

ANISEED The anise plant, a member of the parsley family, has feathery leaves and small, crescent-shaped seeds that boast a sweet, licorice flavor. Used both whole and ground, the seeds add their distinctive taste to breads, pastries, and cookies.

ANISE LIQUEUR A strongly flavored distilled spirit enjoyed throughout southern Europe, where it is produced under various names, including *anis seco* in Spain, pastis or Pernod in France, *ouzo* in Greece, and *anesone* in Italy. Infused with the licorice-like flavor of green aniseed, the liqueur appears in recipes and aperitifs.

ARUGULA Also known as rocket or Italian cress, this delicate leafy green has a peppery, slightly bitter flavor that adds complexity to salads. Its assertive flavor and bright green color also make it a favorite addition to sauces and soups. Look for small, crisp leaves that show no wilting or yellowing.

ASPARAGUS Early spring brings the first wild asparagus spears to open-air markets, an eagerly awaited event all across Spain. The long stalks are actually the shoots of a plant in the lily family, harvested while still young and tender. Most arrive at market bright green in color, varying from slender pencil-sized stems to jumbo stalks ¾ inch (2 cm) thick. White asparagus is grown away from light to blanch it to a pale ivory color and create a more delicate flavor. Wash asparagus spears well in plenty of cool water to remove excess sand in their tips.

BOTIFARRA See page 40.

CANSALADA The dry mountain air of northern Catalonia is well suited for preserving foods, a factor that has contributed to making the region a celebrated source of the charcuterie that plays an important role in Spanish cuisine as a whole. Literally "salted meat," cansalada is the local version of bacon. Any cured fatty bacon, in particular one that is not smoked, can be used in its place.

CASSOLA The thick walls of this round, shallow earthenware pan, also known as a *cazuela,* allow foods to cook gently and evenly. Ideal for long, slow cooking in the oven, the orange terra-cotta of a *cassola* is traditionally glazed only on the inside surface. Season a new *cassola* by immersing it in water for 6 hours. Repeat this soaking occasionally if you live in a dry climate or if you plan to use the pan over the direct flame of a stove top (although it is not recommended for use on the stove top). To prevent cracks, do not heat the pan while it is empty, limit the temperature to very low for its use on the stove top, and avoid temperature extremes.

CAVA See page 56.

CHESTNUTS These treasured nuts grow in the regions surrounding the Pyrenees, where during the autumn months, you can purchase the fresh, hot, starchy-sweet delicacies from street vendors. Cooked and canned chestnuts are available, but fresh ones are worth the extra bit of work needed to remove the tough mahogany-colored shells.

SHELLING CHESTNUTS: To remove the shells, cut a shallow X into the flat side of each nut, then immerse them in boiling water or roast them in a 350°F (180°C) oven for about 15 minutes. Working with a few nuts at a time while keeping the others warm, peel back the points of the X to remove each chestnut's meat. Peel off the thin, beige inner skin and discard. If any nuts cool before you peel them, simply return them to the hot oven or water until their shells warm and soften again.

CHICKPEAS Also known as garbanzo or ceci beans, these nutrient-rich legumes are a staple in many Mediterranean cuisines. The round, beige beans are rich and nutty in flavor, and their firm texture holds up well to long cooking. Rinse and drain canned chickpeas well before using.

CHICORY Pleasantly bitter in flavor, members of the chicory family of greens take well to heartier salads and light cooking. Escarole has wide, flat leaves and pale white stalks loosely gathered around a green-yellow heart. Also known as broad chicory or Batavian endive, escarole can be chopped and tossed in a salad or stirred into soups and pasta sauces. Curly endive, a close cousin of escarole, has narrow, spiky, finely curled leaves and a creamy white heart. With its more delicate texture, it appears primarily in salads tossed with a simple vinaigrette. Although available year-round in most markets, both are at their peak during the winter season. Select crisp, compact heads free of any wilting or discoloration.

CHORIZO There are countless variations on this distinctive Iberian sausage. Made of air-dried pork and heavily spiced with garlic and paprika, chorizo sausage has a rich, smoky-sweet flavor with a hint of tanginess. Each region has its own special style, which may be mild or spicy, fresh or cured, air-dried or wood-smoked. There are two basic categories of chorizo: sausages meant for cooking and those cured for eating uncooked, although some versions can be eaten both hot and cold. In the kitchen, chorizo is most often used in small amounts as a flavoring, adding depth to stocks, sauces, fillings, tortillas, eggs, and bean dishes. Versions from Spain tend not to be as spicy-hot as Mexican-style chorizo, but the latter may be used as a substitute.

COCA, COQUES Small, pizzalike savory pastries that are a specialty of the Costa Blanca and the Balearic Islands south of Barcelona. *Coques* feature a variety of toppings such as tomatoes and peppers, olive oil and anchovies, eggplant (aubergine), or dark greens and caramelized onions.

COGNAC A brandy distilled from grapes grown specifically in the district of Cognac in France. Aged a minimum of 2 years in oak casks, Cognac brightens the flavor of pâtés and is often used to flambé stew meat after browning.

EMBOTITS Cold meats that have been cured according to Spain's long tradition of artisanal charcuterie. Highlighting the central role pork plays in the country's cuisine, a selection of *embotits* might include a pork loin cured with peppercorns, a finely textured ham, paprika sausage, or a special Catalan blood sausage (see page 40).

ENTREPÀ, ENTREPANS Literally "between bread," an *entrepà* is the Catalan interpretation of Spain's much-loved *bocadillo* sandwich. Traditionally enjoyed as a snack during the afternoon or late at night, *entrepans* are popular fare in bars and snack shops. Minimalist in nature, most *entrepans* have simple fillings such as *tortilla de patatas,* a basic egg omelet, fresh goat cheese, or spicy chorizo sausage.

FAVA BEANS From springtime into summer, gardens throughout Spain yield profuse crops of fava (or broad) beans. As the long, wide pods grow older, the inner skin on each bean thickens. Select small pods for the tenderest fava beans, and blanch older beans to help in removing their tough skins.

FIDEO Called *fideu* in Catalonia, the only region in Spain where pasta is widely used, these very thin, vermicelli-like noodles appear in a local version of paella. Fideo is also used in a variety of soups, stews, and vegetable dishes. Look for small bags of the pasta in Spanish or Latin American markets, or use the thinnest possible angel hair pasta you can find, broken into short lengths.

FISH The coastline of southern Catalonia allows easy access to the Mediterranean's abundant fish and seafood.

GROUPER Called *mero* in Spanish and *anfós* in Catalan, this fish thrives in the sea's warm waters. A thick-bodied fish with firm, flaky meat, grouper is superb roasted, grilled, or gently braised.

MONKFISH Often compared to lobster for its rich, white, firm, and finely textured flesh, monkfish is prized by Spanish cooks. Called *rape* or *rap* in Spanish, it is excellent poached, broiled, or grilled.

JAMÓN SERRANO See page 40.

MAHÓN See page 60.

MATÓ See page 60.

MONGETES DEL GANXET Large, white, kidney-shaped beans prized in Catalonia for their smooth texture and thin, delicate skin. The beans absorb flavor well when cooked with sausage, ham, rabbit, or lamb. Look for jars of *mongetes del ganxet* in Spanish markets, or substitute with cannellini, Great Northern, or white kidney beans.

MORTAR AND PESTLE Many aromatic ingredients, such as garlic, release more of their oils when crushed between the surfaces of a mortar and pestle than when cut in a food processor or blender. Look for a generously sized marble or stone bowl when selecting a mortar, to allow easier and more efficient crushing. A proper *allioli* or *romesco* sauce, some Catalans would insist, is best served right in the rough-hewn mortar in which it was made.

MOSCATEL Also called muscat; see page 57.

NYORA PEPPERS Also known as *ñora* peppers, these are essential in an authentic *romesco* sauce. Grown mainly in Catalonia, plum-sized *nyora* peppers lend their red color, sweet flavor, and mildly spicy heat to numerous local dishes. To prepare the dried peppers, cover with boiling water and soak for 10 minutes, then scrape the flesh from inside the skins. Dried ancho chile peppers can be substituted.

PAELLA PAN Spain's famous rice dish is traditionally cooked outdoors in a wide, shallow metal pan placed over a fast-burning wood fire. Made of rolled steel and sporting two round handles, a paella pan can measure from 10 inches (25 cm) to more than 3 feet (1 m) across. A 12- or 14-inch (30- or 35-cm) pan easily fits three to four generous servings. Paella pans should be seasoned and cleaned like woks and cast-iron pans: avoid using soap when washing, dry thoroughly, and then coat with a thin film of oil before storing.

PANCETA Made from the thin, flat belly cut of pork, *panceta* is a streaky bacon often used in the beginning of cooking to flavor sauces, soups, and stews. Substitute Italian pancetta or any other cured, unsmoked bacon.

PARMA HAM This air-dried, unsmoked ham has long been a specialty of Parma, a province of northern Italy. Made from pigs raised on a diet of chestnuts and whey, the finely textured ham has a sweet, nutty flavor much like Spain's serrano ham.

PASTISSERIA, PASTELERÍA For a midmorning or afternoon *merienda* snack, Spaniards will visit a pastry shop to savor tea or coffee with one of their favorite sweets. Named *pastisseria* in Catalan and *pastelería* in Spanish, each pastry shop offers a delectable selection of both sweet and savory snacks, including breads, pastries, and candies.

PASTIS See anise liqueur.

PÂTÉ A classic appetizer in France, pâté is essentially seasoned ground (minced) meat cooked gently in a fat-lined terrine or inside a pastry crust. Its texture can vary from coarsely chopped mixtures, known as country-style pâtés, to silky-smooth spreads.

PERNOD See anise liqueur.

PICADA A Catalan sauce based on ground nuts, typically almonds or hazelnuts (filberts). Thickened with toasted bread and flavored with garlic, saffron, paprika, parsley, vinegar, or wine, a picada gives rich body and depth of flavor when stirred into a stew. Some, much like Mexico's mole sauces, include bittersweet chocolate.

PIMENTÓN Spanish paprika, finely ground from dried nyora peppers (see left), can be sweet, bittersweet, or spicy hot. Look for pimentón in small tins in Spanish or specialty markets, or use sweet paprika in its place.

PINE NUTS The small, pale seeds of certain varieties of pine trees, with an elongated, tapered shape and a rich, sweet, slightly resinous flavor. Used often in southern European and Middle Eastern cooking, pine nuts appear in savory dishes such as salads, stuffings, and sauces as well as in baked goods and desserts. Toast them for about 10 minutes in a 325°F (165°C) oven to bring out their nutty flavor.

PORT A sweet fortified wine produced by adding brandy to partially fermented red wine. Neighboring Portugal, most notably the Douro Valley, produces the most renowned Ports, although Port-style wines are also made in many other countries. Single-year vintage Ports are the finest. Pale tawny Ports, blended from several vintages, may be aged in wood for up to 40 years and are good for both drinking and cooking. Ruby Ports, generally the least expensive, are aged in wood for 2–3 years.

QUESO FRESCO DE BURGOS A fresh sheep's milk cheese produced in Castile-Leon, a province in the north of Spain. Made in 2- to 6-lb (1- to 3-kg) cylinders and often including some cow's milk, this very fresh, rindless cheese, mild in flavor and white in color, is very popular served with fruit for breakfast all across Spain.

RIBEIRO A wine region located in rugged, rainy Galicia, in the northwestern corner of Spain. Ribeiro's vineyards produce fresh, light white wines that are nearly always served young, within 2 years of bottling, to accompany fish and seafood.

RICE Brought to Spain by the Moors, rice became an important crop in the marshlands of southern Spain, where shorter-grain japonica varieties thrive. Calasparra and Valencia rice, medium-short-grain varieties, and Bomba rice are still considered the best for paella. Connoisseurs of Spanish rice refer to its *perla*, the pearl of starch at each grain's core that soaks up the flavors of other ingredients. Italian Arborio or Carnaroli rice is the closest equivalent.

ROMESCO A classic Catalan dipping sauce thickened with almonds, olive oil, and bread. Wine vinegar and garlic round out its flavors, while local *nyora* peppers lend a red color and a touch of heat. Some versions include hazelnuts (filberts), pine nuts, tomatoes, or spicy chiles. Rich and pungent *romesco* accompanies a wide range of dishes, such as roasted potatoes, seafood, rabbit, asparagus, or grilled green (spring) onions.

SAFFRON Known as *azafrán* in Spain, this spice takes its name from the Arabic word for "yellow," evoking the bright hue it lends to dishes. Saffron threads, the dried stigmas of a purple crocus flower, are still gathered by hand, one reason the spice is comparatively rare and costly. Introduced to Iberia by the Moors, it has become a signature seasoning in Spanish dishes, particularly paella.

SALCHICHÓN See page 41.

SARSUELA Also called *zarzuela,* this seafood specialty is served along the Catalan coast. Cooks combine a variety of fish and shellfish—whatever is particularly fresh on any given day—and add wine, tomatoes, saffron or paprika, and ground almonds or bread crumbs to make a brightly flavored stew.

SERRANO HAM See page 40.

SHERRY Sherry takes its name from its place of origin, Jerez, a region of southwest Spain where Phoenician settlers first introduced grape vines. Blended and fortified, sherry wines fall into several styles. Dry or very dry *fino* has a straw color and a delicate flavor that makes it ideal for tapas.

Manzanilla, a lighter, bitter wine, is *fino* produced in the seaside town of Sanlúcar de Barrameda. It pairs with shellfish particularly well. Amber-hued Amontillado is a medium-dry wine with a rich, nutty flavor that complements smoked meats and cheese. Medium-sweet Oloroso develops a dark mahogany color and walnut flavor; serve it with sausage, nuts, or dried fruits. Sweet cream sherry is a dessert wine.

SOBRASSADA See page 41.

SOFREGIT Many Catalan recipes start with this basic preparation. Although Catalan cooks add ingredients like tomatoes, bell peppers (capsicums), garlic, carrots, or paprika, the essential combination remains that of onions and olive oil. *Sofregit* adds a distinctive sweet-savory flavor to Catalan cuisine. Other regions of Spain refer to it as *sofrito.*

SQUID See page 48.

SUQUET A traditional Catalan seafood stew. One of the most popular versions combines fish, clams, potatoes, and tomatoes in a broth that has been thickened with ground almonds and flavored with paprika.

TOMATOES Tomatoes were first cultivated in Spain during the early sixteenth century. In Spanish kitchens, the narrow, firm plum (Roma) tomato predominates, for its deeper flavor and its ability to hold up to long cooking.

PEELING AND SEEDING TOMATOES: Cut a shallow X in the blossom end of the tomato. Immerse in a pan of boiling water until the peel begins to curl away from the X, about 30 seconds. Transfer to a bowl of ice water to cool, then peel away the skin. To seed, cut in half crosswise and squeeze each half gently to dislodge the seeds.

TUNA When buying canned tuna for Spanish dishes, look for imported albacore tuna packed in olive oil. Its richer flavor and texture are essential in preparing certain dishes from southern Europe. If imported tuna is not available, use white albacore tuna packed in water. After draining it well, drizzle 2–3 tablespoons of extra-virgin olive oil over the tuna and set aside for 5 minutes.

VI RANCI See page 57.

INGREDIENT SOURCES

EL CELLER CATALÀ

Catalan *cava*, white, and red wines, including Penedés, Priorat, Montsant, and Alella.

+ 34 977 638436

www.wwwinecellar.com

EL PANTAR

Arroz Bomba Illa de Riu is the highest quality Spanish rice, produced in limited quantities and much sought after by Spanish chefs.

+ 34 977 450594; + 34 977 451711 (fax)

email: elpantar@teleline.es

FORMATGERIA LA SEU

Artisan cheeses from Catalonia.

+ 34 93 412 65 48

www.formatgerialaseu.com

IGOURMET.COM

Spanish cheeses, chorizo, olive oil, ham, and rice.

(877) 446-8763

www.igourmet.com

THE SPANISH TABLE

Spanish food, wine, and cookware, including Catalan cheeses, *nyora* peppers, *botifarra* sausages, serrano ham, chorizo, beans, vinegars, olive oils, paella pans, and terra-cotta *cassolas*.

(510) 548-1383

www.spanishtable.com

TIENDA.COM

Spanish cookware and specialty food items such as chorizo, paella ingredients, spices, cheeses, and olive oil.

(888) 472-1022; (757) 566-9603 (fax)

www.tienda.com

WINE.COM

Spanish and Catalan wines.

(877) 289-6886

www.wine.com

INDEX

A

Alella, 56

Allioli, 105, 185

Almonds
  musician's dessert, 173
  and pine nut cookies, 80
  romesco, 121
  toasting, 173

Anchovies, 49, 79
  escarole salad with salt cod, olives,
    and, 109
  sandwiches with fresh cheese, roasted
    peppers, and, 79

Aniseed, 185

Anise liqueur, 185

Aperitiu, 87

Arugula, 185

Asparagus
  about, 185
  garlic and spring vegetable
    soup, 106

B

Bacallà. See Salt cod

Beans. *See also* Chickpeas; Fava beans
  mongetes del ganxet, 186
  two-course mixed stew of meats,
    vegetables, and, 153

Béchamel, 129

Beef, braised, with
  mushrooms, 138

Beer, 87

Berberechos, 37

Bonbons, 68, 69

La Boqueria, 25–26

Boquerones en vinagre, 36

Botifarres, 39, 40

Bread
  flat-, with eggplant, peppers,
    and olives, 76
  sandwiches with fresh cheese, anchovies,
    and roasted peppers, 79
  tomato-rubbed, 75

Bull, 41

C

Cabbage
  mashed potatoes and, 114
  and pork bundles, 130

Cabra amb pebre, 61

Cakes
  chocolate truffle, 174
  hazelnut, with licorice, 178

Calamars, 36, 48

Calçots, 121

Caldereta, 142

Cannelloni, feast-day, 129

Cansalada, 185

Cargols, 37

Cassola, 185

Catalana, 41

Cava, 56, 181

Chardonnay, 56

Cheese
  and honey with figs, 169
  making, 58
  sandwiches with anchovies,
    roasted peppers, and, 79
  shops, 58
  tart, Ibiza goat, with mint, 177
  varieties of, 60–61, 186

Chestnuts
  roast duck with raisins and, 154
  shelling, 185

Chicken
  baked rice with sausage, chickpeas, and, 145
  braised, with shrimp, 149
  feast-day cannelloni, 129
  and ham croquettes, 92
  roasted, with garlic, 146

Chickpeas, 185
  baked rice with chicken, sausage, and, 145
  two-course mixed stew of beans, meats,
    and vegetables, 153

Chicory, 185

Chocolate, 66–69
  bonbons, 68, 69
  cream, 174
  truffle cake, 174

Chorizo, 185

Clams
  berberechos, 37
  vegetable and seafood noodles, 162

Cognac, 185

Cookies, almond and pine nut, 80

Coques, 64, 185
  de llardons, 65
  de recapte, 76
  de vidre, 91

Crema catalana, 170

Crème caramel, 182

Croquetas, 37

Croquettes, chicken and ham, 92

Cuisine, Catalan
  contemporary, 15–16, 19
  by geographical area, 27–29
  history of, 13–15
  influences on, 15–16, 83, 101, 129

Custards
  Catalan burnt cream, 170
  crème caramel, 182

D

Dessert wines, 173

Duck, roast, with raisins and chestnuts, 154

E

Eggplant, 102
  flatbread with peppers, olives, and, 76
  roasted vegetable salad, 118
  salt cod with peppers, onion, tomato, and, 141
  stuffed, 102

Eggs
  spinach omelet with tomato sauce, 126

Embotits, 39, 41, 185

Empanadas, 84

Entrepans, 79, 186

Escabetx, 88

Escalivada, 118

Escamarlans, 48

Escarole salad with salt cod, anchovies,
  and olives, 109

Escórpora, 49

Escudella, 153

Esqueixada de bacallà, 36

F

Fava beans, 186
    Catalan-style, 113
    garlic and spring vegetable soup, 106
Feast-day cannelloni, 129
Fideo, 186
Fideuà, 162
Fiestas, food-related, 109, 121
Figs, fresh cheese and honey with, 169
Fish. *See also* Anchovies; Monkfish; Salt cod;
    Sardines; Tuna
    shellfish and mixed meat paella, 137
    species of, 49, 186
    vegetable and seafood noodles, 162
    whole, baked in salt, 161
Flam, 182
Formatge de cabra enoli d'oliva, 61
Fuet, 40

G

Garlic and spring vegetable soup, 106
Garrotxa, 61
Gazpacho, 101
Granita, "liquid," of sparkling wine, 181
Grouper, 186

H

Ham
    Catalan salad, 122
    and chicken croquettes, 92
    feast-day cannelloni, 129
    varieties of, 37, 40, 186
Hazelnuts
    cake with licorice, 178
    musician's dessert, 173
    romesco, 121
    toasting, 173
Herb oil, 158
Honey
    about, 169
    and fresh cheese with figs, 169

I

Ibiza goat cheese tart with mint, 177

L

Lamb chops, stone-cooked, with herb oil, 158
Lentil soup, cream of, with garlic-herb
    croutons, 125
Llonganissa, 39, 41
Lobster soup, 142

M

Mahón, 60
Majorcan summer salad, 105
Map, 30–31
Mar i muntanya, 149
Markets, 25–26
Mató, 60
Meats. *See also individual meats*
    mixed, and shellfish paella, 137
    mixing seafood and, 149
    two-course mixed stew of beans, vegetables,
        and, 153
Mercat de Sant Josep, 25–26
Monas, 174
Mongetes del ganxet, 186
Monkfish, 186
    medallions, thyme soup with, 110
    shellfish and mixed meat paella, 137
Mortar and pestle, 186
Moscatels, 54, 57
Mushrooms, 117
    braised beef with, 138
    oven-roasted wild, with garlic and parsley, 117
Musician's dessert, 173
Mussels, 48
    shellfish and mixed meat paella, 137
    vegetable and seafood noodles, 162

O

Oils
    herb, 158
    olive, 43–45
Olives
    escarole salad with salt cod, anchovies, and, 109
    flatbread with eggplant, peppers, and, 76
    harvesting, 44
    oil, 43–45
    spicy marinated, with pickled vegetables and
        garlic, 87
Omelet, spinach, with tomato sauce, 126

Onions, grilled green, with *romesco* sauce, 121
Orada, 49

P

Pa amb tomàquet, 75
Paella
    pans, 186
    shellfish and mixed meat, 137
Panceta, 186
    Catalan-style fava beans, 113
    country-style pâté, 83
    mashed potatoes and cabbage, 114
Panellets, 80
Pasta
    feast-day cannelloni, 129
    fideo, 186
    two-course mixed stew of beans, meats,
        and vegetables, 153
    vegetable and seafood noodles, 162
Pastisseries, 62–65, 186
Patatas bravas, 36
Pâté
    about, 186
    country-style, 83
Peaches, pork loin with, 150
Peas
    garlic and spring vegetable soup, 106
    shellfish and mixed meat paella, 137
Penedès wines, 56, 57
Peppers
    flatbread with eggplant, olives, and, 76
    Majorcan summer salad, 105
    nyora, 186
    roasted vegetable salad, 118
    roasting, 79
    salt cod with eggplant, onion, tomato, and, 141
    sandwiches with fresh cheese, anchovies, and, 79
    and tuna pie, 84
Pernil ibéric, 37
Pernil salat, 40
Picada
    about, 13, 19, 186
    recipes, 117, 126, 157
Pimentón, 186
Pine nuts, 186
    and almond cookies, 80
    sweet pastry with, 91
    toasting, 186

Pork, 39. *See also* Ham; *Panceta;* Sausage
 and cabbage bundles, 130
 Catalan-style fava beans, 113
 country-style pâté, 83
 feast-day cannelloni, 129
 loin with peaches, 150
 stew with picada, 157
 stuffed eggplant, 102
Port, 186
Potatoes
 mashed, and cabbage, 114
 patatas bravas, 36
Priorat, 57

Q

Queso fresco de Burgos, 186

R

Raisins
 musician's dessert, 173
 roast duck with chestnuts and, 154
Restaurants
 with authentic Catalan cooking, 20
 by geographical area, 27–29
 noted, 14, 19, 20
 seafood, 23, 25
 trend-setting, 23, 27
 variety of, 14–15, 19–20
Ribeiro wines, 187
Rice, 187
 baked, with chicken, sausage,
  and chickpeas, 145
 shellfish and mixed meat paella, 137
Rioja, 56
Romesco, 121, 187

S

Saffron, 187
Salads
 Catalan, 122
 escarole, with salt cod, anchovies,
  and olives, 109
 Majorcan summer, 105
 roasted vegetable, 118
Salchichón, 39, 41
Salt, 161
Salt cod, 36, 46, 141
 with eggplant, peppers, onion, and tomato, 141
 escarole salad with anchovies, olives, and, 109

Samfaina, 141
Sandwiches with fresh cheese, anchovies,
 and roasted peppers, 79
Sardines
 about, 49
 fried, in vinaigrette, 88
Sarsuela, 46, 187
Sausage
 baked rice with chicken, chickpeas,
  and, 145
 Catalan salad, 122
 Catalan-style fava beans, 113
 varieties of, 39, 40, 41, 185
Seafood. *See also individual seafood*
 importance of, 46
 mixing meat and, 149
 restaurants, 23, 25
 shellfish and mixed meat paella, 137
 varieties of, 48–49
 and vegetable noodles, 162
Sherry, 187
Shrimp, 48, 95
 braised chicken with, 149
 griddled, with garlic and parsley, 95
 shellfish and mixed meat paella, 137
 vegetable and seafood noodles, 162
Snacks, 34, 91
Sobrassada, 41
Sofregit, 130, 187
Soups
 cream of lentil, with garlic-herb
  croutons, 125
 garlic and spring vegetable, 106
 gazpacho, 101
 lobster, 142
 thyme, with monkfish medallions, 110
Spinach omelet with tomato sauce, 126
Squid, 36, 48
Stone-cooked lamb chops with
 herb oil, 158
Suau de Clua, 61
Suquet, 46, 187

T

Tapas, 34, 36–37, 73, 101
Tart, Ibiza goat cheese, with mint, 177
Thyme soup with monkfish medallions, 110
Tomatoes, 187
 Catalan salad, 122

gazpacho, 101
 Majorcan summer salad, 105
 peeling and seeding, 187
 roasted vegetable salad, 118
 romesco, 121
 -rubbed bread, 75
 salt cod with eggplant, peppers, onion,
  and, 141
 sauce, spinach omelet with, 126
 shellfish and mixed meat paella, 137
 stuffed eggplant, 102
 sweet pepper and tuna pie, 84
 vegetable and seafood noodles, 162
Tou dels Tillers, 60
Trempó, 105
Trinxat, 114
Tuna, 187
 escarole salad with salt cod, anchovies,
  and olives, 109
 and sweet pepper pie, 84

V

Veal
 stuffed eggplant, 102
Vegetables. *See also individual vegetables*
 salad, roasted, 118
 and seafood noodles, 162
 spring, 113
 spring, and garlic soup, 106
 two-course mixed stew of beans,
  meats, and, 153
Vi ranci, 57

W

Walnuts
 musician's dessert, 173
 toasting, 173
Wine bars, 52
 Wines. *See also* Port; Sherry
 DOs for, 52
 history of, 50–52, 55
 making, 54, 55
 sparkling, "liquid" granita of, 181
 varieties of, 52, 56–57, 173, 181, 187
Wine shops, 52

X

Xató, 109

ACKNOWLEDGMENTS

Paul Richardson would like to thank Edwina Taeger, Marc Taeger, Ana Valls, Joan Graells, Juan Ignacio Trives, Maria Teresa Pire, Marlena Spieler, Pepa Aymamí, Pep Palau, Christian Escribà, Jordi Alzina, all the folks at La Boqueria market, and the people of Barcelona in general for their helpfulness and good humor. *Gràcies a tothom!*

Weldon Owen wishes to thank the following individuals and organizations for their kind assistance: Desne Ahlers, Quentin Bacon, Dan Becker, Carrie Bradley, Brooke Buchanan, Ken DellaPenta, Elisabet der Nederlanden, George Dolese, Jean-Blaise Hall, Karen Kemp, Celeste Carrasco Moreno, Joan Olson, Scott Panton, Gilles Poidevin, Eric Ryan, Sharon Silva, and Karin Skaggs.

Weldon Owen would also like to extend their gratitude to the individuals and the owners and workers of restaurants, bakeries, shops, and other culinary businesses in Barcelona and Catalonia who participated in this project: Abac, Barceloneta restaurant, Bar del Pi, Bar Pinotxo, Boix de Cerdanya, Botifarreria de Santa Maria, Brunells, Cal Estevet, Cal Isidre, Cal Pep, Cansaladeria Alsina, Carme Bufí, Carmelitas, Clara Guasch, Clos d' l'Obac winery, Comerç 24, DAF, El Celler Vell, El Xampanyet, El Nou Celler, Els Pescadors, El Taller, Escribà, Espai Sucre, Estrella de Plata, Eulàlia Torres in La Seu d'Urgell, Formatgeria La Seu, La Boqueria, La Casa del Bacallà, La Pallaresa, La Vinya del Senyor, the olive oil producers of La Bisbal de Falset, Oriol Balaguer, Pla de Palau, Quimet & Quimet, Restaurant Sant Pau, Salero, Santa Maria, Set Portes, Tèxtil Cafè, Tot Formatge, Vinacoteca, and Xocoa.

PHOTO CREDITS

PHOTOGRAPHY LOCATIONS

The following Barcelona and Catalan locations have been given references for the map on pages 30–31.

OXMOOR HOUSE, INC.

Oxmoor House books are distributed by Sunset Books
80 Willow Road, Menlo Park, CA 94025
Telephone: 650-321-3600 Fax: 650-324-1532
Vice President/General Manager Rich Smeby
National Accounts Manager/Special Sales Brad Moses
Oxmoor House and Sunset Books are divisions of
Southern Progress Corporation

WILLIAMS-SONOMA, INC.

Founder & Vice-Chairman Chuck Williams

THE FOODS OF THE WORLD SERIES

Conceived and produced by Weldon Owen Inc.
814 Montgomery Street, San Francisco, CA 94133
Telephone: 415-291-0100 Fax: 415-291-8841

In Collaboration with Williams-Sonoma, Inc.
3250 Van Ness Avenue, San Francisco, CA 94109

A Weldon Owen Production
Copyright © 2004 Weldon Owen Inc.
and Williams-Sonoma, Inc.

First printed in 2004
10 9 8 7 6 5 4 3 2 1

ISBN 0-8487-2853-X

Printed by Tien Wah Press
Printed in Singapore

WELDON OWEN INC.

Chief Executive Officer John Owen
President and Chief Operating Officer Terry Newell
Vice President International Sales Stuart Laurence
Creative Director Gaye Allen
Publisher Hannah Rahill
Business Manager Richard Van Oosterhout

Series Editor Kim Goodfriend
Editor Heather Belt
Editorial Assistant Juli Vendzules

Associate Creative Director Leslie Harrington
Art Director Nicky Collings
Designer Nicky Collings, Marisa Kwek
Map Illustrator Scott Panton
Photo Researcher Liz Lazich

Production Director Chris Hemesath
Color Specialist Teri Bell
Production and Shipping Coordinator Todd Rechner

Food and Prop Stylist Ana Torróntegui Salazar
Food and Prop Stylist's Assistant Amanda Laporte
Breysse

A NOTE ON WEIGHTS AND MEASURES

All recipes include customary U.S. and metric
measurements. Metric conversions are based on
a standard developed for these books and have
been rounded off. Actual weights may vary.